Frae a the Airts

Verses by
Allan J. Ramsay

Allan J. Ramsay

carn
PUBLISHING

First published in Great Britain 1996

ISBN 0 9518128 2 3

Published by
Carn Publishing,
Lochnoran House,
Auchinleck,
Ayrshire,
KA18 3JW.

Printed by
Walker & Connell, Ltd.
Hastings Square,
Darvel,
Ayrshire,
KA17 0DS.

Allan J. Ramsay

Allan James Ramsay was born at Brae Lodge Cottage, Auchendrane, on the banks of the River Doon, on 12th December 1909. He moved to Annbank district in the winter of 1912-13 where he later attended Annbank School. However, due to ill health throughout his childhood, he spent a great deal of time on his grandmother's farm, Monkwood Mains, and so also went to Minishant School. He left school at fifteen and joined his father who had a sawmill business at Annbank. At seventeen he very quickly learned to drive a solid tyre five tonner Halley lorry, which became very well known all over Ayrshire, delivering stobs, paling and other products of the sawmill.

In 1930 Allan started a livestock haulage business and became well-known in all the markets from Glasgow in the north and as far south as Stranraer. His first float was a Reo Speedwagon.

In 1937 he married Marion Robson, his schoolgirl sweetheart. She died five months before their Golden Wedding day was due. They had no family.

In 1945 he was advised to at least semi-retire, so he sold the haulage business and moved to a cottage near Ochiltree where he was an agent for Molassine Meal for many years. He attended Ayr market every Tuesday and any other days that sales were on, where he collected accounts for Patterson, Grain Merchants, Kilmarnock.

After moving into Ayr to live, he found many of his farmer friends didn't like attending the market, so he took on the job of selling cattle or sheep for them. He was the last man out of the old market, and he made a speech at the opening of the new market. Knowing the countryside so well and having such a marvellous rapport with farmers, he was persuaded into the job of sheep wintering, and at the ripe old age of 87, he's still doing it.

Betty Rees (née Ramsay)

Bonnie Gallowa'

O' to stray doon in the Glenkens,
Viewing Corserine and Craignaw,
By the Carlin's Cairn, and by the Loch o' Dee.
There the muse is like the mountains,
O' this bonnie Gallowa',
For the mind it is inspired, through een that see.

O' to wake up at the dawning,
And to hear the skylark's lay,
As on wings he trills his music to the skies,
Or at sundown scan the shieling,
On the lonely heather braes,
It is joy to see the peat reek rise.

When the pairtin' 'oor has chappit,
And we a' maun tak' the gate,
May the shepherd lead us safely to oor bield,
And, like Milton, we'll be lichtsome,
Though we only watch and wait,
Till we meet another nicht - A fond fareweel.

The Fishin' Flee

A fellow in a boat wi' me,
Was fishin' wi' a fancy flee,
Wi' colours braw baith black and yellie,
And hairs pu'ed oot a badger's belly,
Whaur did he get that flee sae bonnie?
He got it frae a freen and cronie.
The sportin' shops - they never stock it,
The maker's name is Bobby Crockett.
He used to be a water bailie,
Got feathers aff a capercaillie,
This day we baith were feelin' caul',
This flee caught yin while on the trawl,
He caught it by the dorsal fin,
But sportsman-like flung it back in.
Sae freens if fishin' is your hobby,
You'll need tae get a flee frae Bobby.

Jim and I and the Caravette

It is, I know, the angler's dream,
To dwell beside the loch or stream,
Such dreams I reckoned could be met
By purchasing a caravette.
Hence, in this gadget I invest,
And straightway figure out a test,
In all decisions, small or big,
Some hero acts like guinea pig;
Take great men, like explorer Scott,
Or Yanks, who act the astronaut,
We've got to get boys, void of fear,
Adventurous lads to volunteer,
Guys that will stick through thick and thin,
And, in the end, will surely win,
That, uncomplaining, work and toil,
And fry their ham and eggs in oil,
I have the man to grind my axe,
Exempt, forby, of pay-roll tax,
Therefore, at once, I contact him,
"What would I do without you Jim?"
Oh yes, of course, he did agree,
We'll go the morn and fish Loch Dee,
This Caravette with towing bar
We hitched to my small Morris car,
All fixed in style, just what you want,
My friend I get at Minishant,
We hit the trail for Clatteringshaw,
Among the hills o' Gallowa',
Beside some trees, in sheltered biel'
We bide, and scoff an evening meal,
There, by the sun's last flickering rays,
We silently tak' aff oor claes.
Inside, you see, the space is nippit,
You're best ootside till you get strippit.
We're in, and quietly cuddled there,
We thocht it was a great affair,
But soon began tae hotch wi' pain,
The bed was solid, like a stane.
We turned and tossed the hale nicht thro'
And listened tae a damned cuckoo.
Besides, oor tore banes sair and scaddit,
We baith were caul', we thocht we'd had it,
Sae, as the wildfowl of the glen

Seeks cover frae the haunts o' men,
We are the ither wey aboot,
We're yappin' that we're wantin' oot.
That Summer mornin' it was dry,
The sun rose brightly in the sky,
Altho' we hadn't slept all night,
The air had stirred oor appetite.
Jim, with the pan, at once agrees,
Tae cook the eggs and sausages.
Thence tae the fishin' we maun hi',
Tae catch the morrow mornin's fry,
We view the distant loch o' Dee,
And wash oor face in Garrarie,
There, where the crystal water's free,
We dicht the bleers frae ilka e'e,
Surrounded by the towering hills,
We soused the water roon oor gills,
On scenes like these I ponder now,
While yet the streamlet cools my brow,
And count the blessings I possess,
No valuator can assess.
Land of bog myrtle and of peat,
My dear dream valley of retreat,
Lang may we baith be spared tae see,
This weil lo'ed scene aroon' Loch Dee.
That day eight troots were in the net
When we returned to Caravette,
We hitched her on and thence did beat
For Gatehouse, on the River Fleet
Where once a shepherd's cottage stood
We parked, in perfect solitude,
We set oor table neat and trig,
Wi' tattie crisps and potted pig,
The midges, they were by the hunner,
And sookin' bluid frae saint and sinner,
A plastic poke, just napper size,
Nae doot took midges by surprise,
They seemed to fasten fast on Jim,
His poke was just too wee for him,
Like spacemen, we were chewin' fruit,
Still fankled in oor parachute.
The table cleared and both well fed,
We topple into little bed,
At three A.M. I wake once more,
Terrific rain pelts on the door,

At nine A.M. Jim says to me,
"Are you no' ready for a pee?"
Says I, "I'll bear it with a grin,
Lie doon, forget, and cuddle in."
But Jim's distress was really dire,
He slippit oot in nicht attire,
His troosers wet, his jacket wetter,
"Ach weil," says he, "I'm feelin' better."
At 2 P.M. I must admit,
I'd truly had enough of it,
And, when I'm oot, before we dee,
I'll get some eats for you and me,
Hence, in the car all high and dry,
Two whipped cream walnuts I espy,
Two slice of date loaf, one bridge roll,
A tin o' pears, tho' somewhat droll,
For breakfast and for lunch 'twill do,
Thereafter feel as good as new.
This Caravette could be a boon,
To couples on their honeymoon,
But, for two lads, not bent on such,
We felt like rabbits in a hutch,
Or banties in a chicken coop,
In fog and rain, like thick pea soup,
Just like the prodigal langsyne,
Wha ett the husks meant for the swine,
We truly tae oor senses came,
And wondered, "Why left I my hame?
Please help me don my pants, I pray,
My shirt, my socks, my jacket tae,
And a' the acts for me you've din,
I'll pey ye back tenfold tae ane."
Thus, wi' oor togs and shin completed.
We faced the gale and swiftly beat it,
Richt doon the road tae "Cruachan",
Where hams and eggs aince mair we scan.
I'm shair we'll never camp again,
For Summers here are maistly rain,
Sunshine for lang we never get,
And sae, I've selt the Caravette.

They Cannot Read Their Tombstone

We ne'er heed our friends devotion,
Lest, perhaps, we show emotion,
And to speak our thoughts we seem to have a fear,
So we never sing their praises,
Till they're pushing up the daisies,
But then, alas, our friend's no longer here.

Though their friendship's really wanted,
We just take it all for granted,
To show them how we feel we never try,
We may more or less ignore them,
Till they're gone, - then we adore them,
And eulogise their virtues to the sky.

If your friends are worth preserving,
And you think they're praise deserving,
Then don't just keep the thought within your head,
But tell them loud and clearly,
That you like them most sincerely,
For they cannot read their tombstones when they're dead.

When we find a friend despairing,
Who may feel no one is caring,
Then you can give the help that he may crave,
Right away's the time to do it,
Or later, you may rue it,
For he can't get your assistance from the grave.

For dead friends, we've flowers of splendour,
And the word that's kind and tender,
While the air of loss and sympathy we breathe,
But the right time for the giving
Of the flowers, is when they're living,
For they cannot smell the blossoms on their wreath.

Ne'er assist in friends detraction,
If your heart wants satisfaction,
But extend the hand of fellowship instead,
Let them know though fame neglect them,
That you honour and respect them,
For they cannot read their tombstones when they're dead.

The Cat

It happened in the month o' May,
At Tannockhill, up Mauchline way,
A mairret couple there you'll find,
Wha are extremely good and kind,
There's Willie and his wife ca'd Bet,
The ither day they had the vet,
Tae doctor up a certain coo,
That Willie thocht had chronic flu,
The vet took oot his wee black bag,
And gaed the coo a dandy jag,
He said it would be swift and sure,
And would reduce her temperature,
Then Betty with the vet did chat,
And told him of her pussy cat,
She told him Jimmy was his name,
Because he often gaed frae hame.
(I ought tae state, these friends o' mine,
Their ferm is by the railway line.)
Well Jimmy was a right good sport,
He courted cats of every sort,
He paid his visits every night,
And slept by day to keep him right,
Alas, one morning plodding back,
He had to cross the railway track,
That night he'd truly had enough,
He'd met so many bits of fluff,
And, feeling tired, and somewhat seedy,
He crossed the line, no' quite sae speedy.
Sad to relate, ere he got clear,
An engine melts him on the rear,
He hirples home and there he lay,
No more to venture far away,
He did not fancy milk or meat,
But hung around and licked his seat,
The tabby cats all missed their master,
And guessed he'd met with a disaster,
An odd one came that had the fever,
But Jimmy never gied his beaver.
Still Jimmy rallied, never mind,
Except for lump on his behind,
It grew as big's a turkey egg,
High up on Jimmy's aff hin' leg,
This story Bet got off her chest,

And vet took in with interest.
"I'll see this cat right now," says he,
"Though quite a problem this may be.
These lumps on cats I truly hate,
And though I've seen me operate,
It's seldom that I have success,
They mostly pack in, more or less,
And then, the cost, - the mair's the peety,
It's no' worth spendin' on a cheety."
He studies cat, and strikes a plan,
"Do you by chance know any man,
That carries with his other gear,
Those rings that make a bull a steer?
Or, for the little lambs that skip,
That mak' a wether o' a tup?
A man that does such work complete,
This cat would be right up his street,
He'd do it for a few odd bob,
And make a really lovely job."
Thus vet with Betty ends the chat,
He's managed rid of this Tom cat.
Hence, - Willie 'phones me, re this question,
Explaining fully vet's suggestion.
He made me plainly understand,
This ticklish job that was on hand,
Fine Willie knew, at all events,
I carried these accoutrements,
He'd seen them lying in my kit,
And, - once a quey with extra tit
He'd watched me square, down to the core,
And left her with the usual four.
I said to Willie, "Right ma son,
I'll be the morn at half past one."
As shin's the dinner 'oor was din,
At Tannockhill I landed in,
Oh Willie started off tae say,
He didna' ken richt whit tae dae.
"This job," he said, "has many dangers,
Because the cat is feart for strangers."
Says I, "If that's the case, tae Hell,
Can you no' dae the job yersel'?
I'll show ye hoo tae work the thing,
And hoo tae fix your rubber ring,
And dae the deed wi' care and skill,
And stroke the cat, and keep it still."
Hence Betty goes and cries its name,

And, sure enough, pair Jimmy came.
She brings him in the gairden gate,
Where Willie's gaun tae operate,
Then Willie speaks and strokes its fur,
And Jimmy sterts tae purr and purr,
His tail was upright in position,
He didnae ha'e the least suspicion,
Willie was crawlin' on his knees,
And Betty went for bits o' cheese,
She said it was his favourite dish,
Except, of coorse, for dauds of fish.
I was inside the hoose ma lane,
And lookin' through the window pane,
Oh Jimmy's lips were fairly smackin',
And Willie's fairly gettin' crackin',
He's got it ower the lump right now,
Hell! Jimmy's bolted - meow-wow-wow,
He's pu'd machine oot Willie's haun,
Oh Heavens! Whaur is this he's gaun?
He's birlin' this wey, then reverse,
Wi' gadget danglin frae his erse,
Says Betty, "This is something chronic."
Tae me, it was perfect tonic.
Wi' lauchin' I was in a fit,
My very sides were like tae split,
The frantic feline's in a fix,
And doing acrobatic tricks,
Willie, tae grab him, tried wi' pluck,
But Jimmy saw his dirty luk,
And kent that he was better free,
And hid ahin' an aipple tree.
I thocht my tool was gone for smush,
Till Jimmy gaed a frantic rush,
Oot through the hedge, among the hey,
And that was whaur the thing gaed wey,
Oh I was awfu' pleased masel',
Tae see the instrument had fell.
Says Willie, "Will this prove success,
Or maybe in a richt dampt mess?"
Says I, "According to the rule,
You've done the job most beautiful."
After a blether, and a crack,
Says I tae them, "I'll hit the track."
I noticed by the hedge's root,
Pair Jimmy's whiskers stickin' oot,
Says I tae Betty, "Just mak' shair,

The rubber ring is still on there."
She cried, "Cheet - cheet," but Jimmy he,
Just backed and bucked aboot a wee,
He wadna' come up tae her haun',
Tae let her see the rubber baun',
But, as he turned, she noticed it,
Was absolutely in its bit.
I've been wi' Willie on the 'phone,
Tae hear hoo Jimmy's lump got on,
Says he, "It's oor firm estimation,
A most successful operation."

Reply to a Lass who Mentioned I had said the Wrong Words

Dear Lass, I read your poem through,
Your accusation's very true,
At real Burns' nichts, where Rabbie shines,
You must sing all the proper lines.

The first verse, sure, you ought tae sing,
"A cup o' kindness," just the thing,
The "willie waught" is at the en',
Och naw, we didna' need it then.

I really think at pairties, Jean,
It's nicer tae say "trusty frien'",
A willie waught's best left alane,
Especially if you're drivin' hame.

"We'll meet again some ither nicht,"
I ken it's wrang, but hope it's richt,
A later poet - (never me),
Thocht he wad chinge the words, ye see.

He said, "Dear Cronies, every guest,
Sing, Meet again, and a' the best,"
When haudin' haun's, and, in a ring,
It's a' yin wan, Jean, whit ye sing.

The Black-Face Breed

Fond o' the Scottish hills and dales,
Fond o' the sheep and cattle sales,
Fond o' auld Nature through and through,
Fond o' hill herds, sae staunch and true,
My thochts, must needs, oft times return,
Tae loch and valley, hill and burn,
Whaur Covenanter's blood was shed,
Lang syne, happed in a gory bed,
'Mang the bog myrtle and the peat,
Whaur heather bell and bracken meet,
On these same hills, by heighs and howes,
The freendly herds attend their yowes,
I'm thinkin' o' the black face breed,
On Scotia's braes, they tak' the lead,
Braw black faced sheep can bate them a',
Especially doon in Gallowa',
Odd lads in Ayrshire, pals o' mine,
No' faur frae Gallowa's border line,
Like "Grimmet", wi' his famous stock,
A credit tae we, Ayrshire folk.
The same applies the Barrhill airt,
Aye mentioned at the auction mairt,
But Galloway withoot a doot,
Is always there or there aboot,
The Newton Stewart ram sale ring,
Gars kilties dae a hielan' fling,
When they hae had a richt guid dram,
A ten poun' note's no' worth a damn.
An' efter a' that's why they came,
Tae tak' a black-face ram back hame,
Back tae their croft awa up by,
E'en tae the bonnie Isle o' Skye,
Nae question, this will dae some guid,
Tae get the prime o' black-face bluid,
The Gallowa' boys, weil kent by name,
Don't want to winter hoggs at hame,
Like Alex Campbell and his sons,
Wha like guid broth and coffee buns,
Supplied here by the N.C.B.
Nane better by the Cruives o' Cree,
Or Andrew Graham frae Irelandston,
Wha rings me often on the 'phone,
I tell him, aye pit on twa keels,

For fermers here in Ayrshire feils,
Frae first October's Autumn blaw,
Till end o' Mairch wi' rain and snaw,
They put on flesh and growth o' horn,
Though whiles their fleece gets scutched and torn,
An odd yin, as a braxy dees,
An odd yin, in a wife's deep freeze,
Anither's hunted wi' a dug,
Has mair than eil stobs oot its lug,
It's very throat is gapin' wide,
Wi' wool torn oot frae side tae side,
I'm sorry, aye, I must confess,
Tae see braw sheep in sic a mess,
These are the risks a man must tak'
Aye hopin' that they'll a' come back,
Fu' weil I ken the ups and doons,
As black-face hoggs gang roon their roons,
O' world-wide sheep this black-face breed,
Can, wi' the best, haud up the heid,
And Scotland's shepherds o' the glen,
To me, are Nature's Gentlemen.

Scotch Words

(Ongauns gang gyte)

We whiles like tae meet in Ayr's auld farrant toon,
Tae hae a bit crack, and a dance, and birl roon,
When ye're ettlin' tae gang, syne, ye canna weil get,
Ye're taigled thro' some loon no' steekin' the yett.
The nowte hae sneaked oot, when the sneck wasna in,
And some auld yowes were staunin' jist ready tae rin,
I was gie sair forfochen, and ready tae greet,
And the rime aye got whiter, like hauf frozen sleet,
A' roon the dyke back there was glaur oxter deep,
Nae won'er the kye rake, the stots and the sheep,
I got late tae the dance, had a blether or twa,
My dress was a' clarty - no' bonnie ava,
I felt ocht but weil buskit, I was sorry I came,
When I heard the knock chappin' I daunert back hame.

The Shape That I'm In

There's nothing, dear Doctor, the maitter wi' me,
I'm joggin' along and as fit as can be,
I've arthritis, nae doot, in baith o' ma knees,
An' aye when I talk, I talk wi' a wheeze,
My pulse is gie wake, and' my bluid is gie thin,
But I'm no' bad ava, for the shape that I'm in.

Airch supports I hae got for baith o' my feet,
Or I wadna be able to walk on the street,
Soun' sleep is denied me each nicht I lie doon,
My memory's fadin', my hert's in a swoon,
My heid is whiles sair, An' I'm awfu near blin',
But I'm no' bad ava, for the shape that I'm in.

My stomach seems frail, sae I don't eat a lot,
I was thinkin' yestreen that the flu I hae got,
Sae I'll tak' a wee dram, and an aspirin the nicht,
And trust I'll be fine at the break o' daylicht,
The best cure o' a' is tae keep up your chin,
For I'm no' bad ava, for the shape that I'm in.

Noo, when I was a lassie my slippers were blue,
I could kick up my heels like a horse at the ploo,
I can scarce toddle noo tae the toilet and back,
And my auld buffs o' slippers are coloured jet black,
I scan each day's "Herald", the obits I aye read,
If my name is no' there, then I ken I'm no' deid,
And thankfu' I am, I'm still able tae grin,
Naw, - I'm no' bad ava, for the shape that I'm in.

To Hugh and May, "Rigghead"

On their Golden Wedding

It is with pleasure warm and true,
I write these lines to May and Hugh,
Noo fifty years ha'e slippit roon,
Since May had on her waddin' goon,
Hugh, withoot doot, I truly ken,
Is one o' Nature's Gentlemen,
Fu' mony tares we've had indeed,
Aroon' the steadin' o' Rigghead,
At waddin's o' this family tree,

We've been at mony a jolly spree,
Wi' toasts tae bridesmaids, unco braw,
In summer's suns and winter's snaw,
I've seen them whiles in scanty hose,
And whiles row'd up like Eskimos.
This nicht there's hosts o' near relations,
And mair than that - fower generations,
Burns said, thro' this world faur and wide,
"Nae man can tether time nor tide."
And sae life's story does unfold,
How health's worth more than much fine gold,
And joy, and love, and peace forby,
What all great fortunes cannot buy,
It is for you, dear Hugh and May,
These priceless gifts I would convey,
And, may what lies ahead be cheer,
Like happy days o' yesteryear.
God's blessings on this golden pair,
Sincerely yours, - A freen frae Ayr.

The Romagnola Bull

Up on the hillside at Craigskean,
Where all the fields are fresh and green,
A Surgeon lad and I ae day,
Were seekin' beasts that went astray.
John Kerr had tried me on the 'phone,
Tae tell me, they were at Knockdon.
Hence, when we met I heard him say,
"This grazin' will be hard to pay."
Says he, "If they're in dacent shape,
I'll buy them, if the price is chape."
"You twa," says he, "Wad rin and rin,
And maybe never get them in."
Hooever, let us gang the noo,
And see this bonnie calf and coo,
This six month calf last week I ta'en,
Richt up by Stirling tae Dunblane,
The champion ticket fair and square,
We brocht it back wi' us tae Ayr.
The Surgeon says, "Hoo wad it dae.
To swap oor twa wee beasts for thae?"
John luked at him and gaed a grin,
"Ye wadna' like a dug flung in?"
"Then I've a bull you'll like nae doot,

A great big kin' o' ugly brute,
A Romagnola type they say,
It's neck's a' black, it's body grey."
We thocht the beast wad hear the soun',
And maybe gie a wee luk roon,
Insteed, what dae ye think we saw,
It's face caught by the underjaw,
Between twa bars, I ask ye why,
Certainly no' wi' bullin' kye.
John caught it by the nose and broo,
And gaed its heid a double screw,
A sicht like this I've sometimes seen,
Calls for a clout atween the e'en,
It staggered back, as richt as rain,
He'll no' try that daft trick again.
The moral is - In work and deed,
Don't ever get a big swalt heid.

A Gentleman's Thoughts

when landing at Prestwick on a 'plane from America.

Can you imagine what I saw,
A little space and it was gone,
A thrill inspired my mind with awe,
The mystery of the morning dawn.

I sat within that flying 'plane,
And gazed into that heavenly sky,
I saw a star through glints of rain,
And quietly murmured, "What am I?"

I landed near the banks o' Doon,
Where dear immortal Burns was born,
Somewhere betwixt the sun and moon,
My dream fled, in the early morn.

I simply pondered what this lad
Of words and wisdom might have penned,
What influence would the "Muse" have had,
From break of day, till journey's end.

To Tom and Winnifred Howie

of Downieston, March 1985.

Dear Tom, it really is a shame,
Tae ken your wife is far frae hame,
You're bound tae fret, - it's only human,
For Winnie is a clever woman,
She never would have been selected,
Had she not had the gifts expected,
You've guid freens in your fellow men,
Like John Sykes and his pal, aul' Ben.
On lassies never cast an e'e,
Unless you want a cup o' tea,
For flashy dames o' ilka group,
Can only land ye in the soup,
There's Billy McIndoe, I ken,
Could fix ye wi' a cloakin' hen,
But better far tae gang tae "Picken",
And get a pack o' frozen chicken,
Ca' Smithston wife up on the 'phone,
And get a mealy tattie scone,
Or gang tae Mrs. Welsh doon by,
And nab a bit o' rhubarb pie,
Auld Smithston is a sure retreat,
Tae fix you up a bite o' meat,
Then herd yer flock and tend yer kye,
And days and nichts will sin slip by,
This separation in your life,
Will strike you - hoo you miss your wife,
At Downieston she'll soon appear,
Tell her you love her most sincere,
Here's health and joy beyond compare,
To Tom and Win in ample share.

To Laura Goodwin

on passing her special Nursing exam with an extra plus.

Dear Laura, you're my favourite lass,
You've gained this extra special pass,
It gladdened me to hear the news,
And wakened my poetic muse,
Two loving kisses sealed apart,
I hold for you, my fond sweetheart,
I'm your great uncle, Laura dear,
And you're my choice - NURSE-OF-THE-YEAR.

Grace Before Meal

given to Davie Purdie.

For happiness and friendship here,
We thank you Lord, for this sincere,
For food, of which we now partake,
We give you thanks, for Jesus' sake.

Birthday Greetings

to Bob Logan, 1st June 1990.

I pen these lines, dear friend to you,
With every blessing, warm and true,
Count all the joys of auld lang syne,
I often dream and ponder mine,
It is such thoughts in many ways,
That see us through the present days,
May peaceful hours aye follow through,
In all the little jobs you do.

A Grace for the Carrick Club

(Young Farmers)

This Carrick Club a race has run,
Now fifty years since it begun,
We see these tables neatly spread,
Thus, - giving us, our daily bread,
A milestone here on Life's Highway,
Grant us your blessing, Lord, we pray.

To Roger Goodwin

capped at Glasgow University, 6th December 1991.

Congratulations through and through,
This card is sent with pride for you,
Good luck and joy in all you do,
        And hear and say,
And aye look out for something new,
        On Life's Highway.

Dedication to my late dear friend, Robbie Murray

and to the now-deserted cottage where he was born.

My heart with pleasure always fills,
When traikin' o'er the heather hills,
Alas, - a sadness struck me when,
High up, beyond the Forrest Glen,
A dear deserted hallowed spot,
Had vanished, - like a passing thought,
Dear Robbie Murray's kith and kin,
Were born and cradled safe within,
Never again I'll knock this door,
Or tread the flagstones on the floor,
I've drank the cup o' kindness sweet,
When all this family was complete,
Wi' braw oatcakes and Stilton cheese,
Before the plantin' o' the trees,
The fiddle strains have died away,
That Robbie Murray used to play,
The couthy crack and rhyming skills,
Are scattered o'er the Dungeon Hills,
I've still a shepherd's crook to show,
That Robbie fashioned long ago,
A masterpiece of wondrous art,
A gift I'll treasure in my heart,
I'll miss the cottage, - truth to tell,
I'll miss the friends I loved so well,
The sinking sands have sank for me,
Till time unveils eternity.

Rabbie Burns

Entered in a competition, Sunday Post, 24th February 1992.

Where Bonnie Doon rins wimplin', first licht o' day I saw,
Ae December in a hamely but and ben,
Twa or three miles frae the cottage whaur, 'mid Jan'war's sleet and snaw,
Was born the pride o' Ayrshire's famous men.
For frae every neuk and cranny o' the lands across the sea,
There are hearts that dearly lo'e oor Scottish lore,
Sae be prood my freens o' Scotland and your Ayrshire pedigree,
Though you wander to a distant foreign shore.

It is wi' joy I linger by ilk bonnie bank and brae,
Wi' thochts o' Rabbie Burns, - his works sublime,
Aye remembering we are merely dust, and made from common clay,
Leaving footprints on the golden sands of time,
For oor poet surely struck the chord o' genius, firm and sure,
And he lo'ed the lassies fondly, this we ken,
But don't forget thro' his short life, he measured rich and poor,
And he wrote, "I dearly love my fellow men."

Brocht up on simple hamely fare, wi' Scottish haggis fed,
And parritch warm tae fill the wame forby,
The songs he wrote are joy to hear, like "Scots wi' Wallace bled,"
And poems, - tales o' horses, sheep and kye,
I visit oft the Ayrshire haunts where Rabbie tilled the soil,.
At Mauchline ferms, baith Lochlea and Mossgiel,
I cast my thochts tae yesteryear o' hardy rustic toil,
When Clydesdales turned the sod o' ilka dreel.

Withoot a doot, the road was stey, that you had whiles to tread,
At biggin' stacks o' corn you had the knack,
The tracks were rouch and grim and dour, but you were country bred,
You plodded on, and never lookit back,
This world is altered, (maybe no'), - the folk that bide therein,
They are the culprits o' the change we see,
It's no' the honest love we knew, aft noo defiled in sin,
I think Dear Rab, you'd think the same as me.

The pills, the drugs, the condoms, are inventions now we see,
They were never ever kent in Rabbie's day,
I ask you to consider this, sincerely wise and true,
Is it, - the brains o' man? or Nature's Way?
The answer some day will be shewn, in letters plainly seen,
With Robert Burns we'll read it, you and me,
Appearing there, before "The Judge", behind the mystic screen,
When "Faither Time" unveils eternity.

To Mrs Bentley

with best wishes, December, 1975.

Here by the firelight's fading gleam,
In fancy, oft times there, I dream,
I wander by the loch or stream,
In sunshine fair,
Macaterick's islands ever seem,
To lure me there.

My mind most surely sheds a ray,
On Ballochbeatties, by the way,
Here, Mrs. Bentley plies her tray,
O' guid Scotch fare,
She caters, thro' the live long day,
Wi' pride and care.

Dinner at seven, on the dot,
Gigots o' lamb, or rump o' stot,
Here, on the bell she'll quietly trot,
Custards and cream,
Comes sailin' in tae feed the lot,
Each fishin' team.

Sae, Mrs. Bentley, fond and true,
I send good wishes, lass, to you,
May you be like the auld herd's coo,
And still dae weel,
Aye keep the fishers' bellies fu',
O' milk and meal.

O' Ewes and Tups

O' ewes and tups I've seen a few,
O' Blackface rams and Leicesters blue,
I've seen some dampt queer folk forby,
And great big bulls and calving kye.
The nicht we'll talk o' ewes and hoggs,
And rams and herds and collie dogs,
And dour auld fermers, hard as nails,
When selling stock and making dales.
Hence freens, the nicht there's some in here,
Are maybe straught, but blooming queer.
Ae day ane bocht some ewes in Ayr,

At twa and twenty poun' and mair,
MacWhirter was a needfu' case,
Wi' ne'er a smile upon his face.
The auctioneer he tried again,
But chapped them doon - "Laigh Alticane,"
Donald stood in the passage there,
And met the seller fair and square,
He said, "Intae yer pooch get stuck,
And howk me oot a wee bit luck."
The boys at Newton Stewart toon,
The market staun's aside the Croon,
This was the "Croon" o' a' ram sales,
Nae place in a' the world excels,
This very year o' seventy two,
A record price for blackface 'oo,
Six thoosan' and three hundred quid,
Is chappit doon tae Knockicoid,
Grimmet, the seller, stood his grun',
Says he, "I bred him just for fun."
There's mony gie strange market tales,
At Newton Stewart's famed ram sales,
But, wait for this, and this is true,
There's no a sheep, or bull, or coo,
In Newton Stewart, or in Ayr,
Can match life's freenships anywhere,
In freenship's name, strong is the tie,
What pounds and pence can never buy,
Aye buy guid stock, keep bullocks braw,
But prize guid freenship, maist o' a'.

A Ninetieth Birthday

A ninetieth birthday, this is why,
We're lookin' back on days gone by,
But forward we maun cast and e'e,
And reckon wi' the yet tae be,
May health and peace from Heaven sent,
Be yours, dear Grace, and sweet content,
These wishes heartfelt and sincere,
Are sent with love for you my dear.

Spring

The winter quietly creeps away,
New Spring-born lambs, they dance and play,
The sunshine stretches day by day,
        Oor wee birds sing,
I welcome them in every way,
        Hail, - glorious Spring!

Epitaph on Hugh Boyd

No. I Holding, Yett, Tarbolton.

Fareweel, fareweel, my auld freen Hugh,
The last furr's turned, - laid by the ploo,
Some gie hard graft you wrastled thro',
        Stey braes did speel,
Your kin' are scarce, - they're no' made noo,
        Sleep soun' auld chiel.

Oor Ain Lassies

Think o' the bus, - the conductresses,
The nurses, cooks and air hostesses,
In school, the teachers and dressmakers,
The chorus girls and fancy bakers,
There's shop girls, aye, and smart hairdressers,
Hoose keepers for auld din professors,
Receptionists and majorettes,
Telephonists and usherettes,
Mannequins and typists too,
To mention only but a few,
Nae mother's son, nae mortal man,
Can e'er attempt what lassies can,
Nae wonder Burns through life aye said,
His sweetest 'oor was wi' a maid,
His brightest jewel and his queen,
Was (day and nicht) his bonnie Jean,
Sae, - lo'e a lass wha's mind is bricht,
And aye mak' shair her hert is richt.

The Triumph Acclaim

There's a car on the market,
The nicest I've seen,
It's on sale and inspection,
By Appleyard team,
There are three special models,
And here is the name,
When you 'phone you just mention,
 A Triumph Acclaim.

It is class engineering,
In every detail,
The body's a treat,
Of a very high scale,
The sale lads are clever,
They're smart at the game,
But you'll never be stung,
 With this Triumph Acclaim.

If you own an old motor,
They're certain to buy,
They'll give what will get you,
Some chips and a pie,
But the great thing is this,
You have stepped into fame,
You have left Appleyard,
 With a Triumph Acclaim.

The Rose

(Written 6th October 1941)

Where in the twilight's evening hour,
Beats now the heart I used to know,
Where is the rose within the bower,
That in life's garden used to grow.

Why do I miss that golden gem,
Why was its beauty ever born,
To leave a bruised, a broken stem,
With naught to cherish, but a thorn.

Has Nature in her mystic plan,
By storm and tide, been too severe,

Or, could it be that mortal man,
Perchance has acted insincere.

I'll wait and hope that on life's way,
I'll find an answer to my cry,
I'll always watch, I'll always pray,
That I may find a reason why.

Childhood Memories

He tarried mid his native soil,
His aged steps were slow,
He asked the old folk whom he met,
For friends he used to know.
He traced them quietly, one by one,
For days he had to bide,
Tam taigled him a gie lang while,
Aroon his ingle side.

The crack was guid o' days gone by,
When they were chiels at schule,
They used tae break the maister's hert,
Baith Tam and him, and Bill.
Aye Bill has lang syne slipped awa',
But well we'll min' his worth,
He was, (just as the neebors said),
The plain salt of the earth.

"Noo Tam," says he, "I'll need tae gang,
The 'oor is gettin' late.
I'll drap inby, some ither nicht,
Again, for auld times sake.
But ere, my freen, I do return,
The auld haunts I maun see,
I'll rise the morrow mornin' shin,
Gin God is guid to me."

He toddled back tae whaur that he
Was lodgin', ben the room,
His heid, the bowster scarce had touched,
When sleep cam' ower his croon.
Thence in the mornin' fresh as pent,
Tae Annbank he's awa',
He managed doon tae Tarholm Brig,
He speired aboot Craigha'.

They telt him hoo, that a' thae three,
In turn had got the chap,
Craigha', they lauched, and Tarholm tae,
Were swiped clean aff the map,
But Annbank yonder on the brae,
Rebuilt in a' her prime,
Her fitba' team, did ye no' hear,
Was da'in' weil this time.

The bus of coorse noo tak's him back,
It's great the things that rin,
He used tae walk it, kickin' stanes,
He aye was sair on shin.
Back for anither wee bit rest,
The morn at screch o' day,
He'll dauner roon by Weston Brig,
Tae Gadgirth and Burnbrae.

Ah, there again his boyhood scenes,
Were blotted from the place,
A tear stole from the old man's lids,
And trinkled doon his face.
In fancy, like a web he wove,
The scene he knew so fair,
Awakened by the water's song,
The bonnie banks o' Ayr.

That nicht he did relate tae Tam,
Hoo things were altered sair,
But we of coorse are altered tae,
Oor pows are gettin' bare,
But, nae mair greetin' Tam for me,
The Lord be praised instead,
Wha gave me strength tae see my hame,
Whaur I was born and bred.

The 'Herd's Fair

Dear Shepherds, Fermers, wifes and weans,
A' that hae Scotch bluid in their veins,
I want your freenship, no' your riches,
This nicht you've left your dugs and bitches,
You've left them by a cosy fire,
Or maybe lyin' in the byre,
You've left your sheilin' in the glen,
Tae mingle wi' your fellow men,
And you are welcome, ane and a',
Frae croft, or manor, great or sma'.

I want tae tell you o' some sprees,
That happened by the auld sheep rees,
I min' o' aince a chap ca'd Billy,
Was dippin' sheep nearhan' Glenwhilly,
His wife was there, his weans forby,
Tae help the 'herd, at least tae try,
They did their best wi' willin' spirit,
Till ae big ewe was comin' forrit,
Wi' ae terrific breenge and blatter,
It sent the wife - souse, in the watter.

The 'herd, although he lauched a wee,
Was sorry, sic a sicht tae see,
He hauled her oot, what think ye then,
He squuezed her in the dreepin' pen.
That was a story o' the dippin',
I'll tell ye ane aboot the clippin'.
This really happened, I ha'e min',
Aboot the year o' thirty-nine,
A sturdy fellow, frae the toon,
Had got a job wi' Wullie Broon.

They were a' clippin' there thegither,
Some slow and ithers hell for leather,
This hefty chap had lots o' pluck,
And intae this auld ewe got stuck,
Determination's bound tae win,
He rammed the shear whiles in her skin,
The blood was tricklin' doon his wrists,
He ga'ed the ewe some turns and twists,
And finally he turned it roon,
And sat on it, tae haud it doon.

Wi' micht an main he buckled in,
And swore that he wad see it din,
Sune doon his cheeks the sweet was rinnin',
The boys a' roon' were fairly grinnin',
He rose and shouted, "Rise ya stumer,"
And this, ma freens is no' a rumour,
It never rose, - he gruped its heid,
"Tae hell," says he, "The blighter's deid,
Is that no' just a perfect scunner."
Says Wullie, "Mutton, for your dinner."

Grace

Given at New Cumnock Herds Fair.

Good Shepherd, may this nicht be yin
O' fellowship and freendly crack,
Forgie us Lord if we should traik,
A kennan whiles frae off the track.
Bless a' the busket tables spread,
Wi' hamely fare, - oor wames tae fill,
And guide us when the haunshake's by,
Safe tae oor bucht, ayont the hill.

The Late G.M. Lockhart

of Stair House, January 1961.

He lived.
The way of human life he knew,
He battled oft to win his plan,
He saw important problems through,
He kept the faith, - a common man.

He worked.
Time, held appointments all the way,
But aye with humour beaming there,
He gave his work by night and day,
And oh, he loved the House-o-Stair.

He died.
One night he said, "The hours are slow,
I've an appointment from on High,
I cannot wait, - please let me go,
'Tis in the Palace of the Sky."

To Miss Hutchison, Newarkhill

To sit beside a mountain stream,
May stir the muse, or cast a spell,
The water's song makes memory dream,
Where love and pleasures ever dwell.

To think of friendship sweet and true,
Oft makes my heart with joy o'erflow,
At Newarkhill I'll think of you,
A friend indeed, so good to know.

Another

No friendship frail, no friendship fleet,
No idle fancy of the heart,
We knew but one delight, to meet,
We felt but one regret, to part.

Life's Treasure Trove

Some day I'll come by hill and glen,
And bide a wee beside Loch Ken,
And visit ilka but and ben,
    For auld lang syne,
That's hoo I long my time tae spen',
    The pleasure's mine.

If Allister and Mary's there,
Their cosy hame I'd like tae share,
Just for an oor, or maybe mair,
    Same crack tae ca',
And stories I could tell that pair,
    Then slip awa.

And, as I travel, what I've told,
Shines in my mind like letters bold,
Earth's fortunes must in time grow cold,
    Life's treasure trove
Is founded, not on wealth of gold,
    But fondest love.

Lines

As you walk o'er life's broad highway,
You encounter hills that are long,
    But with courage stout,
    You must all step out,
And show the world we are strong.
And though you feel in danger,
With hope you will struggle through,
    And friendly smiles,
    Will shorten the miles,
And you'll feel as good as new.

You may dwell in the halls of pleasure,
There's friends galore to meet,
    If you stroll along,
    In the busy throng,
Or tramp the busy street,
Do try and help your neighbour,
Fling open wide the door,
    For you never know,
    How life may go,
In the days that lie before.

Take time on the lonely hillside,
Away from storm and strife,
    By the pebbly stream,
    Take time and dream,
On the beauty of love and life,
And tend to your own heart's garden,
And give it your constant care,
    And watch, and wait,
    By the garden gate,
Your friends will see you there.

Be brave when you meet the darkness,
Be staunch and ever true,
    With troubled breath,
    Be firm till death,
Someone depends on you,
For to stain a love so tender,
You will fail in God's main test,
    And in some quiet part,
    You will break a heart,
That always loved you best.

To Hugh Jardine

The year o' Nineteen Sixty-Two,
Is swift and surely wearin' thro',
The Autumn tints o' russet hue,
And fading green,
Gars me write doon my thochts tae you,
My dear lo'ed freen.

My thochts this nicht are whaur ye bide,
Close by your cosy ingleside,
There's cronies whiles frae faur and wide,
Tae ca' the crack,
O' blackface ewes you've shewn wi' pride,
Bred at Marbrack.

Life has been pleasant steyin' there,
Tho' whiles at times ye've shed a tear,
But wi' the springtime o' the year,
Ye'd onward trail,
And a' the time your freens sincere,
Wad never fail.

There's still a lot o' wark tae dae,
Whaur hills are no sae stey, they say,
Noo that yer pow is turnin' grey,
Nae need tae run,
But dauner on a quieter way,
Till set o' sun.

Lines

John Sykes, the first time he's been here,
Has wrocht wi' sheep for mony a year,
And whiles an odd wee bullock tae,
I've seen him buy on market day.

At fifteen month, no' ony mair,
He graded ain doonby in Ayr,
The truth I tell, it is ma son,
That bullock weighed straight half a ton.

Its body was as black's a nigger,
And boys, it had a dandy figur',
Its hips were hefty, like a dame
That's maybe left her steys at hame.

Its brisket was as fat's a bear,
John clipped its back a' clear o' hair,
Its face was white a' ower its skull,
Nae doobt its faither was a bull.

John stepped up tae the auctioneer,
And whispered something in his ear,
In ony case, the hin'most bid,
Was dampt near touchin' Ninety quid.

Reply to The Toast to the Lasses

Sent to Marion Howie in Australia, January 1964.

This honour, freens, conferred on me,
Has gart the saut tear dim my e'e,
Auld Scotland, hoo I lo'e thy name,
The place I always ca' my hame,
In Ayrshire I was born and bred,
On guid plain scones and bannocks fed,
No mony miles, I ocht tae say,
Frae whaur dear Rab saw licht o' day,
The wee thack cottage, weil I min',
Still hauds the scrolls o' lang lang syne,
But nearer still across the fiel',
Was whaur he wrocht aboot Mossgiel,
Nearhan' forby was Adamhill,
And Lochlea, Bennals, Willie's Mill,
These a' were circled in a line,
Roon oor wee hoose, that hame o' mine,
Oh mony were the lasses sweet,
He coorted in Tarbolton street,
Whaur, as a bairn, I learned tae read,
But, efter Rabbie Burns was deid,
And Mauchline was a mere stonethrow,
Frae oor we cot o' long ago,
There, tales o' Pussy Nancy rang,
The Beggar's Howff was always thrang,
A' this dear cronies, at this spree,
Swells noo within my memory,

I thank you sir, with Scottish pride,
Frae a' the lasses faur and wide,
I'm pleased tae hear that noo and then,
We're pretty near as guid's the men,
My thanks is simple, - plain my part,
But spoken with a humble heart,
We'll work awa as we hae din,
Tae mak' this worl' worth leevin' in,
And lo'e ye still whaure'er ye bide,
Tho' mountains, hills, and seas divide.

Fragment

In tenderness this heart has bled,
As pure as Springtime's morning dew,
At evening hour, a tear I've shed,
And prayed in silence oft for you.

Fragment

The hert it is that makes ye richt,
Shed love and joy, by day and nicht,
I judge, no' by the ootward sicht,
        On what I see,
It's what is hidden frae the licht,
        That's dear to me.

Limerick - The Perfect Husband

A man who attends to the chores,
And his own darling wife just adores,
Hates drinking and smoking,
Is never provoking,
And all other women ignores.

Lines

We pay for what we drink and eat,
We pay to have a special seat,
We purchase this for someone's sake,
We sometimes give, we often take,
We buy, we sell, at times we lend,
But how do we acquire a friend?

A friend is never bought or sold,
'Tis love that counts, it is not gold,
The tax on friendship's always free,
It is not marked in £.S.D.
And, write this down, a special note,
Your health, is in the self same boat.

All Nature's beauty's yours today,
No charge to you, no bill to pay,
Just listen to the birds that sing,
This does not cost you anything,
Be thankful that you live and move,
In such a world of light and love.

Deep down, within your bosom's core,
Keep these within your treasure store,
And folks will meet you here and there,
And want to buy your stock and share,
No stock exchange transfers this deal,
'Tis friendship's love is bond and seal.

Marion Howie's Reply to the Toast to the Lasses.

Poem after short speech, January 1965.

Dear homeland I love you, your valleys and glens,
Your rills and your rivers, grey coolins and bens,
The smell o' the peat reek, the scent o' the briar,
The bloom on the heather, my hert can inspire.
My ain bonnie Scotland, you're dearer tae me,
Than lands o' bright sunshine far over the sea,
'Mang hills and 'mong heather, fain noo wad I roam,
Auld Scotland, my country, my birthplace, my home.

My thochts are in Ayrshire, by dear winding Ayr,
Whaur Rab, wi' the lasses, had aye time tae spare,
I noo roam in fancy beside the dear stream,
And gaze frae its banks on the folk o' my dream,
I thank you, dear Sir, frae a hert that is fu',
And frae a' the sweet lasses that list' tae me noo,
We lo'ed Rabbie dearly in days o' lang syne,
Guid-bye dear auld Scotland, frae me, and frae mine.

To Mrs. Burgoyne, Edinburgh.

Whither it be a freenly crack,
Or special ca' that brings ye back,
Whither in ha' or roadside shack,
        I'll meet you there,
E'en by the Trystin' Thorn's kent track,
        I dinna care.

For a Christmas Card

Oftimes I've met the heart of stone,
Rigid and stern, and all alone,
Alone, because it cannot spare,
One spot of love, or friendship share,
I've met the heart that ever tries,
To gain the treasures earth supplies,
And, in the end the best is lost,
Too late, alas, he counts the cost,
For me, the heart I like most dear,
Is simple, open, and sincere,
With wealth, accountants ne'er unfold,
O'erflows with love it cannot hold,
I pen these words, my story's true,
Because I found this heart in you.

A Friend's Wedding in Australia

Sent to Mrs Ormond of High Barley, Gatehouse of Fleet, on the occasion of a friend's wedding in Australia, September 1965.

These lines, sent by the Air Mail Post,
From dear auld Scotland's distant coast,
May illustrate in some small way,
The fondest greetings they convey,
For, fond they are indeed, my dear,
And Scotland always is sincere.

The day has dawned, may bells ring true,
Proclaiming joy and love for you,
Tina and Harry, now made one,
Have, on this day, a quest begun,
May health, throughout this journey be,
The mainstay, and, the golden key.

Winds of adversity may blow,
But, hand in hand, determined - slow,
Together, whom the heart beats true,
No wind, or tide can sever you,
May you look back and always say,
"Oh happy, happy wedding day."

To Chic and Maidie

November 20th 1965.

Dear Chic, it is November chill,
And we're forgethered at Cockhill,
Your job I ken lad, ca's for skill,
        I'm weil aware,
Your mind whiles reels against your will,
        I'm perfect shair.

To lift one heart, despondent, low,
One single heart throughout the show,
Makes, not in vain, your act, although,
        You never knew,
That someone, somewhere, as they go,
        Remembers you.

Hence, it is heartening news to hear,
Appreciative words of cheer,

It covers up the scornful sneer,
        O' polished faces,
Gie me the honest man sincere,
        Nae airs or graces.

But Chic, my boy, your whole career,
Is stayed on this wee lassie here,
For Maidie is the one most dear,
        With whom you play,
The game, with Maidie out, I fear,
        Is thrown away.

Sae, when you hae an oor tae spare,
Relax your brain, and banish care,
And mind there's folks aroon' auld Ayr,
        Baith leal and true,
That wish you health, in ample share,
        Enough for two.

To the Same

To this year's show I've never been,
I meant to go, last nicht, yestreen,
If I had went, I would have been,
        But did not see,
I should have went, I think, I mean,
        The wife and me.

I would have clapped my little hand,
And listened to the famous band,
But didn't go, you understand,
        I'm sorry too,
I disobeyed the wrong command,
        And never knew.

Ayr Toastmasters Club Dinner

29th November 1965.

Dear freens, Toastmasters o' auld Ayr,
My hert keeps singin' in my chair,
Thanks tae ma freen, Bill Thomson there,
'Twas his request,
That, since we baith belang tae Stair,
I'd be his guest.

My thanks to you, Bill, is sincere,
I feel the glow o' freendship here,
Bound, by the fellowship o' cheer,
I'm fond o' this,
Intent, I strain a listening ear,
Nae words tae miss.

Micht I express my wishes true,
Tae ae dear freen and cronie, - Hugh,
Congratulations, sir, to you,
This honour high,
That has been thus conferred on you,
Gold cannot buy.

You did not covet, dream or aim,
To climb this ladder, seeking fame,
But just by character it came,
What better score,
You always, fairly, played the game,
Who asks for more?

The gangrel's curlin' club will be,
Staunin' ye haufs, like cups o' tea,
But fitba' fans, they wadna' see,
They're faur ower thrawn,
But a' the rugby boys, like me,
Will shake your haun'.

To Arthur Haugh, I'd like tae say,
May peace and pleasure bliss your way,
Now President, - I trust and pray,
Your work will be,
In tune wi' members, - rich and gay,
In harmonie.

This 'oor o' freendship here I spen',
In social mirth wi' fellow men,
Stirs up the muse, and guides the pen,
        Thro ilka line,
Sae, frae ma hert I truly ken,
        The pleasure's mine.

To Duncan MacNae

On his retiral, November 1962.

Dear Duncan, I am pleased tae be,
Your guest in sic a companee,
I think you're richt tae rest a wee,
        Noo tae retire,
Frae graip and shovel you'll be free,
        In market byre.

Nae mair tae fash wi' auld ewe sales,
Or wallop bullocks thro' the scales,
Or hark tae dealers makin' dales,
        And whiles indeed,
I ken you've heard the damntest tales,
        And shook your heid.

Nae mair you'll mark doon clips and keil,
Or sheep and kye in ilka fiel',
Baith Donal' Walker and Matt Steele,
        Were just a plague,
You did your best for them as weil,
        As Jimmy Craig.

When I went wi' a float masel',
I've seen you sen'in' me tae hell,
I'd say, "The kye are maistly yel',
        That come frae here,
There's no sae mony, truth tae tell,
        Are fair and square.

"But if you mean tae pey the float,
I'll fetch ye oot the best they've got,
Suppose they're burnt broon o' their coat,
        And clinket too,
You'll get them all, like pies red hot,
        Baith bull and coo."

Then Duncan, whiles I've sent ye hey,
Tae stap the mooth o' coo and quey,
"The price," you'd say, "I wadna' pey,
I'm dampt guid shair,"
And then next time I cam' yer wey,
You wantit mair.

When I luk back this very nicht,
Lang syne I kent your hert was richt,
I judge, a man, no by the sicht,
O what I see,
It's what is hidden frae the licht,
That's dear tae me.

The auld year's swiftly wearin' thro',
We're near the en' o' Sixty-Two,
My wishes are sincere and true,
And aye ha'e been,
God grant guid health and joy tae you,
My dear aul' freen'.

Revd. C.L. Johnstone's Presentation

Silver Jubilee at Auchinleck, 28th March 1966.

Rob Wallace, and his pal, Jim Hall,
Ring up my wife, a local call,
To fix a time appointment, soon,
Some evenin' when the sun's gone doon,
They dinna want tae come on speck,
They dae things richt, at Auchinleck.
My wife arranges, then and there,
Tae come on Sunday nicht tae Stair.
The boys arrived, dead on the nail,
And told an interesting tale,
The main thing was, a special spree,
Their minister's silver jubilee.
Now in these lines let me relate,
Some items, dotted on my slate,
The Revd. C.L. Johnstone, - man,
I'm pleased this nicht tae skae yer haun'.
In 1941, retrace,
You'll min' when first you saw this place,
Called to the helm, the ship to steer,
By faith, this five and twenty year.
Thro' stormy seas o' strain and stress,

Thro' waters calm, of pleasantness,
Yourself, to guide this crew afloat,
With God, the Captain o' the boat.
Noo when ye first cam tae this toon,
Reporters, they were jaggin' roon',
Tae get some first haun information,
Great readin' for the congregation,
Wi' snippets, tracin' a' yer breed,
The Chronicle, were miles aheid,
Thro' trippin' oot ower yin anither,
They grup the portrait o' yer brither,
And shove him heid first in the press,
Wi' hair as black as auld Black Bess.
The congregation were upset,
Tae see this parson, black as jet,
When they'd been telt, or saw nae doot,
Aboot his hair, as white's a cloot.
Thus Auchinleck did ca' the crack,
He canna baith be white and black,
And mair than that, they telt us, shairly,
I wad ha'e min', his name was Chairley,
Well, things got sorted, fair and square,
O' that, each member's well aware.
I'll hiv tae mention in this rhyme,
Aboot his love o' pantomime,
He's written script for mony a show,
For well up in the teens, I know,
And strange, but true, I won't say why,
He also fell in love forby,
And, - like all stories old and new,
Got married, and his children - two,
Some pantomimes need held in check,
Especially here, at Auchinleck.
The loves o' Mr. Johnstone's store,
Are listed here, there's many more,
Thro' a' the country far and wide,
There's dear auld Glesca on the Clyde,
Wull Fyffe's ain sang maun still be true,
He should hae left a bit for you.
To walk, to swim, no better ploy,
To climb the heather hills, is joy,
And then there's hame, what happy scene,
Tae ca' the crack wi' bonnie Jean.
This nicht we walk doon memory's lane,
And link the past, in freendship's chain,

This gift, is but an outward show,
The swelling love lies deep and low,
And no mere words can e'er impart,
The fondest memories of the heart.

Lines Penned to Donald Cameron

After reading his book, - While the Wild Geese Fly, 1985.

A freen o' mine o' Ayrshire breed,
Gaed me a story book tae read,
This fellow Alex Kerr by name,
Kens you, dear Donald, just the same.
Kens a' the country you stravaig,
Glen Nevis braes tae Loch Arkaig,
Frae Spean Brig ower tae Newtonmore,
Herdin' the hoggs, near thirty score,
Wi' dugs and bitches, whiles yer ain,
E'en aince ye threw yin oot the train,
An auctioneer, an honest chiel,
Ye didna like the job too wee,
Ayre drovin' cattle near and faur,
Saw bullocks houghs deep in glaur.

A piper on the barley bree,
At ferm sales won his weil earned fee,
Made a' the fermers, stern and dour,
And thrawn aul' dealers bid like stoor,
You bocht three horses aff the grass,
Went tae the office for a pass,
"D. Cameron is my name," you says,
"You'll get your cheque in twa three days."
"Nae cheque, nae horses," says the guy,
"You've got three horse yersel', - goodbye."
Some nags you cannot yoke them wrang,
While ithers just refuse tae gang,
You get them wadna' pu' a pun',
But staun and champ and kick the grun',
Wi' tummlin-tams they gar ye greet,
An' feert for motors in the street.

Wi' cattle, mony a drovin' spree,
"The lowing herd winds o'er the lea",
Fort William is a Heilan' toon,
A picture in the month o' June,
Braw gairdens, floors o' ilka hue,

And greens, fresh wi' the mountain dew.
Some hoose prood wifes at crack o' dawn,
Look oot the windy at the lawn,
And Lord Almichty whit they spy,
Is three or fower big heilan' kye,
"That aul yin fegs will pay for this
They're Cameron's - I'm shair they're his,
Yestreen I saw them oot the park,
Traikin' aboot afore the dark,"
Aye Donald you are wan aul' deil,
My lawn's ploo'd, like a bloody fiel',
You'll men' your dykes and men' them noo,
And square me what I'm justly due,
Heids aff my floors, and I'm no' kiddin',
This gairden's like a fermer's midden'.

Tourists while toddlin' up the Ben,
Spinnin' ye yarns ye didna' ken,
"Don't drink frae springs, it's no' the ticket,
Tak' it frae hame, fae oot the spiket",
Like you, oftimes I drink my fill,
Frae some clear sparkling mountain rill,
Whiles on a day o' summer's heat,
In shady pools I've cooled my feet,
Again, like you, I never hear,
The corncrake's call o' yesteryear,
Last time I heard that craikin' cry,
At Uig, in the Isle o' Skye,
A bird seen seldom on the wing,
And ony wey, it coulda' sing.

It is indeed my deep regret,
That you and I have never met,
But well and truly lad I ken,
You're one of Nature's Gentlemen.
Dear Donald, here's my honest view,
Your kin' are scarce, they're no' made noo.

The above poem was included in a second edition of While the Wild Geese Fly (1986), and Allan Ramsay and Donald Cameron subsequently met.

Mairburn Farewell

At Mairburn, freen, weil may ye speer,
Whaur's the kent shout, the noise and steer,
When (as a lad) ye hailed Tam here
        Time and again,
The pages noo o' yesteryear,
        Are passed and gane.

Man I hae min' the same as you,
When I wad ca' and lift a coo,
Or maybe some auld twisted soo,
        Tae hurl tae Ayr,
The scene I doot has altered noo,
        For ever-mair.

E'en at his waddin', lang years syne,
I toasted Tam and Grace, I min',
Their health I drank in rich red wine,
        True and sincere,
That self same day I read a line,
        For a' tae hear.

In this auld hoose they aye ca'd hame,
I see my poem in a frame,
And mony times I've gane and came,
        And strange tae say,
A thocht within me wad exclaim,
        "That was a day!"

For fower years past, aye noo and then,
I've turned the caur up this roaden',
Richt thro' the kitchen I'd gae ben,
        I kent the track,
Wi' ane o' Nature's gentlemen,
        Tae ca' the crack.

Noo freen, alas, the haun o' fate,
Has cut the string, and shut the gate,
Has ta'en a cloot, and washed the slate,
        O' pain complete;
He had a patient weary wait,
        But didna' greet.

And sae the noise and steer is gane,
They'll miss him maist that was his ain,
But, be like him and no complain,
        That was HIS wey,
Thus, copy this - a noble gain,
        Frae freen, Tam Hey.

Lines on a Birthday Card

It is with pleasure warm and true,
I write this birthday card to you,
Now ninety years have slipped away,
Since, - Alfred, - you saw licht o' day,
You'll aye look back on memories dear,
The happy days o' yesteryear,
May you have peace, and wear a smile,
Aroon your dwelling at Carmyle,
Take this fond wish with love sincere,
Good health to you, - A guid new year,
You share the date wi' Burns himsel',
The next day, I cam' oot the shell;
(But some years later.) - Let me say,
The twenty-sixth is my birthday.

John Sykes Retiral Presentation

Hollybush House Hotel, 12th March 1982.

This nicht in Hollybush Hotel, it's a very special spree,
Come one and all and join in mirth and social harmonee.
A service presentation, and an anniversary too,
What better could you wish for freens, frae Billy McIndoe.

O' John and Mrs. Sykes dear freens, I'm happy you tae ken,
You are the real salt o' the earth, o' Nature's Gentlemen,
I'll aye keep ca'in at your hoose, tae hae a hamely crack,
And fine I ken I'm welcome there, and the same applies tae Jack.

O' mony bonnie ewes you've kent, and mony dugs forby,
And mony richt guid calves you've had oot o' the guid hill kye.
Ann odd richt calvin' quey you've had, that were stirks you got frae me,
Aye come John whaur ye get the best, and tae hell wi' povertee.

It's six and thirty years the day, since Jean and John were wed,
Tae New Luce went their Honeymonn, that's where they went tae bed,
O' these were the days when folks slept soun, nae cramp in the airms or the legs,
In the mornin' when they wakened up, they were ready for ham and eggs.

O' mony are the ups and doons as on through life we go,
And mony are the freens we've met, the freens so good to know,
When years lang syne we looked ahead our dreams seemed far away,
But looking back the span is short, it's just like yesterday.

Nae doot at times the road was stey, the tracks were rouch and dour,
Ower heighs and howes you had tae plod, and cope wi' sweet and stour,
Noo, may ye toddle on your way in happy freendship true,
Wi' memory's bricht o' this great nicht, in Nineteen Eighty Two.

Kyle (Rhodesia)

I ken oor Kyle in Ayrshire,
And the bonnie Kyles o' Bute,
Rhodesia has a Kyle forby,
A Kyle that I salute,
The braw braw braes beside the banks,
Seem paradise tae me,
With Nature's bird song in the air,
Peace and tranquility.

The freenly crack o' a' aroon,
Gars my fu' hert o'erflow,
Peter and Paul - they played their pairt,
Wi' faces all aglow,
Doon on the lake Dear Bill and I,
We caught a few nice bass.
We voted - (and agreed, we were,)
These lodges are first class.

Noo ere we daunner back tae Ayr,
And Caledonia's shore,
We've packed a host o' memories,
Within oor treasure store,
True thanks sincere tae new freens met,
And, fare ye weil awhile,
And if we're spared again tae flee,
We'll aye come back tae Kyle.

To Davie Raeside - Reply

Dear Davie, freen frae West Mainshill,
Whaur frosts are snell, and win's are chill,
I like oft times tae gie a ca',
Tae see your Ayrshire kye, sae braw,
Your sonsy queys, a weel bred team,
A han'some stock, I think supreme,
Whiles I get Margaret on her own,
And hae a hame-baked tattie scone,
I'm pleased, dear Dave, when you did learn,
Aboot my leg you had concern,
And straight way you contacted Bob,
A first class lad to do the job,
Well I am happy here to say,
My leg is in the bettering way.

Now David Reid, my trusted freen,
His wife is kent tae us as Jean,
Bob Cowie treats her wi' his lamp,
And keeps her legs frae gettin' cramp.

I'll tell ye o' anither Johnnie,
An honest and a trusted cronie.
He's no sae drouthy, on the wine,
A drink o' water suits him fine.
This whisky is a sticky wicket,
Faur chaper, just screw on the spicket.

That's Davie Raeside, - cheery loon,
Returnin' hame frae Miebole toon,
Wi' his pick-up he got a clatter,
His knee got wan richt Hellsfire blatter,
It swalt about the size o' three,
O Davie had a chronic knee.
He went tae Bob I'm telt, next day,
Tae see whit Bob had got tae say.
Says Dave, "Bob, will I be alricht?"
Says Bob, "The chances are, ye micht,
But aye remember, Dave," says he,
"You always wis a bit squee-gee
Tae cut it aff wid mak ye lame,
And wooden legs are no' the same,
Tho' miracles come frae abune,
I think, at least, I'll save your skin."

And a' thro' Bob, I'm pleased to state,
Dave's even tried a roller skate,
Again through Bob's incessant skill,
Dave's still the fermer at Mainshill.

To Johnny Boyd on his Retirement

April 1980.

Dear Johnny lad, my dear lo'ed freen,
I heard a wee bit news yestreen,
That when the month o' April's thro',
You'll lee the tractor and the ploo.
You'll bide at hame and tend your stock,
And dae a turn for ither folk.
An odd bit gairden, 'mong the roses,
Wi' May, next door, and then the Hosies,
Your days o' schule you're bound tae min'
Were by in Nineteen Twenty Nine,
At Onthank, Longhouse, and Crawlaw,
You did hard graft, among them a',
Then Moneyacres changed your life,
You took unto yourself a wife,
You reared six weans, a' braw weil bred,
You must hae had a double bed,
Twa lassies, and fower lads, I ken,
Their hame, aft times, a but and ben,
Come ither moves - baith Pant and Burn,
At Laigh Grange tae you had a turn,
Odd ither places I could name,
Ere to auld Enterkine you came,
Your faither there I weil hae min',
And mony ploys o' auld lang syne,
Noo Johnny lad, change doon a gear,
Since Nineteen Eighty is the year,
Just tak things easy ower at Stair,
And ca' the crack aye here and there,
My wish for you and your dear wife,
Guid health and joy, the best in life,
And mony years yet may ye see,
The best, wha kens, is yet to be.

In Memory of a Friend

My guid auld frien's gane owre the knowe,
He'll find a shelter there,
Near whaur the Lugar Waters rin,
Tae meet the winding Ayr,
Frae that bit bield whaur noo he bides,
There's nane has e'er come back,
And my hert's wae tae think, nae mair
Wi' him I'll get a crack.

For aften by his ingle-neuk,
An 'oor wi' him I'd spen',
While confidences we exchanged,
Aboot the wyes o' men,
And lookin' back we realised,
Hoo greed their lives could turn,
While inhumanity tae man,
Gars countless thoosan's mourn.

For spivs and drones he had nae time,
Or them wha watch the clock,
Nocht in this warl we were agreed,
Is queerer than its folk,
And aye he ca'd a spade a spade,
While words he didna' wale,
When inner passions ance were roused,
They'd pierce a coat o' mail.

His gift for memorising verse,
There's few like him I ken,
Frae rambling rhymers like mysel',
Or Rabbie Burns's pen,
Wi' this, while ill in bed he lay,
His ward-mates he wad cheer,
Saved Doctors drugs, aye, lives as weel,
When daith for some seemed near.

Although on Scotland's roll o' fame,
His name micht no' appear,
This tribute noo I pey that frien',
I've kent nigh forty year.
Just like the ripened grain he fell,
Before the Reaper grim,
This world a better place wad be,
If we had mair like him.

Ayr Cattle Market - the Old and the New

James Craig Ltd. 2nd November 1993.

The year is Nineteen-Ninety-Three,
The leaves are falling from the tree,
Burns spoke about November chill,
He never mentioned Whitefordhill,
This market, new, is stationed here,
Transferred from town this present year,
The old mart, built in days lang-syne,
Established, Eighteen-Eighty-Nine.
James Craig, accept congratulations,
This name, rings out five generations,
I've met them all, plus kith and kin,
Through joy and sadness, thick and thin. .

Well, right now, Whitefordhill's begun,
"The fight is o'er, - the battle's won."
Nae special names I'll mention here,
O' drover, clerk, or auctioneer,
A' freens, on which I could rely,
Aye helpin' me, in days gane by.
I was just coontin' oot yestreen,
Eleven sales rings I hae seen,
In Ayr's auld market, in the past,
I've watched the sales, frae first tae last,
Wi' bulls, and queys, and stirks, and coos,
An' calves, and horses, boars and soos,
Nanny goats, and bearded billys,
Clydesdale men, wi' cowts and fillys,
Christmas buyers, Ayr toon folks,
For turkeys, geese, and bubblyjocks.

In Nineteen-Twenty-Seven, I,
Cam wi' a float, that held three kye,
Wi' solid tyres, a gie rouch ride,
But still, it was my joy and pride.
Mike Craig, he states, without a sigh,
"Nae sadness here, o' days gane by."
For me, a wee tear dims my e'e,
As long as memory holds the key.

A great highlight of long ago,
A Clydesdale stallion stole the show,
Ayr market was the appointed place,

To square a long fought farming case,
Nine thousand, and five hundred more,
Was paid in pounds, - a treasure store,
Nineteen-Eleven, - tell me how,
You count that value, here and now?

For this new market on the brae,
Again, best wishes, I convey,
To all concerned, - wha leeves tae see,
I trust, the best is yet to be.

On the Passing of my Dear Wife

On 11th February 1987, five months short of our Golden Wedding.

Fu' mony are the joys we had,
When life was fresh and young,
The sound of music filled the air,
The songs were sweet we sung,
When love's young dream bestirs the heart,
O'erflowing in a song,
In these blythe days o' yesteryear,
The blood was running strong.

When coortin' by the wee moss burn,
Our love was warm and true,
I recollect these hours o' bliss,
When life and love were new.
The burn still babbles doon the glen,
The channels deeper wear,
The mark o' time is on oor broo,
Since sweethearts, we were there.

Fond memories ever fill my thoughts,
Great treasures rich and kind,
The gifts that gold can never buy,
Are banked within my mind,
And still this constant love remains,
This tribute of the past,
In growing old this is my song,
As long as life shall last.

Birthday Greetings to Mrs MacGregor

100 Years of age today, 9th September 1986. (Fond of Clydesdale Horses)

"Buchlyvie" is a Scottish name,
O' Clydesdale horses, world wide fame,
They named one "Baron", all agree,
A title for his pedigree.
The "Baron o' Buchlyvie", - here,
The wonder horse of yesteryear,
My dear old granny used to tell,
Good stories I remember well,
The "Baron" was a sheer delight,
To listen to in bed at night.
Renowned around the Ayrshire coast,
Deserving many a farmer's toast,
The sale in Ayr was one sensation,
Dunure Mains, then his final station,
His skeleton you still can see,
Within the Kelvin Gallery,
Mrs MacGregor, my dear friend,
These special lines to you are penned,
This story is, to you a thrill,
Related ofttimes at Parkmill,
The good old days of what has been,
Cannot be blotted from our scene,
The golden hours we used to know,
The joys and peace of long ago.

One hundred years since lights first ray,
Shone on you on this happy day,
May peace be yours in rich supply,
And love - the gift that cannot die,
When life's sun sets, earth's long lent lease,
Will pass on to the "Prince of Peace."

While on Holiday in Salisbury, Rhodesia

(after seeing their way of life),
I write these verses for my ain folk, at hame, in bonnie Scotland.

Born by the Ayrshire Carrick shore,
Weel versed and read in Scottish lore,
Rhodesian scenes I now explore,
    But where's the key?
To open up this man made door,
    It vexes me.

I'm certain sure within your frame,
There's bound tae be a glint o' shame,
Oor ain forefathers, faur frae hame,
    In days langsyne,
Helped by Rhodesia, won the game,
    For yours and mine.

Hoo can it be this turn o' tide,
Hoo can ye lee a comrade's side?
The gulf tae me seems far too wide,
    God only knows,
The lads that were oor guard and guide,
    We ca' them foes.

Don't look to names o' high estate,
Don't scan through ranks o' rich and great,
Sit quiet a wee, and watch and wait,
    (A work of art.)
The answer's on the Master's slate,
    Within the heart.

I know for sure I'll never see,
The day when nations all agree,
Droon greed and envy in the sea,
    Make Burns' lines score,
"That man tae man micht brithers be",
    The world o'er.

Charlie Binnie's Spoon

Dear Charlie Binnie, you hae won,
A new horn spoon, your auld yin's done,
Tae fit your mooth, this brand new spoon,
Will slide the porridge quietly doon,
A metal spoon is nae dampt good,
For eatin' body-buildin' food,
This braw new horn spoon, I'll guarantee,
Will feed ye till the day ye dee,
Wi' this swell gift that you hae got,
The stuff will slidder doon yer throat,
Eatin' at mornin' noon or nicht,
Yer erse will only need a dicht,
If you should need a Beecham's pill,
I keep a box at West Mainshill.

Lines to Matt Mundell

Author of Country Diary.

We'd dauner ower the bracken braes,
On bonnie bricht lang summer days,
Some weil kent herds and dugs we'd praise,
　And sheep and kye,
Come hame, whiles tired, wi' gie wat claes,
　In days gane by.

These thochts, o' hikin' on the hills,
By wimplin' streams and mountain rills,
Whaur grows the bent, and heather bells,
　In summer's heat,
My hert at once wi' pleasure fills,
　It gars me greet.

O' Matt I liked your couthy crack,
Tae dot things doon, you had the knack,
We'd shelter shoors in some auld shack,
　Nae oors were drear,
This winter nicht I'm toddlin' back,
　Wi' memories dear.

In Fond Memory of Alastair Gordon, Woodhead

Dear Susan and Elizabeth,
the following lines are taken from Psalm No. 103, they are fitting;

"For He remembers we are dust,
And He our frame well knows,
Frail man, his days are like the grass,
As flower in field he grows.
For over it the wind doth pass,
And it away is gone,
And of the place where once it was,
It shall no more be known."

I have added to the above, in the same rhythm:

Dear Susan, in the "Book of Life",
I see your partner's name,
A gentle shepherd of the flock,
Who always played the game.
I see it here on Memory's scroll,
The scene that love fulfils,
With letters sewn in burning gold,
Across the heather hills.

Mr McQueen's Presentation

Thursday 10th January 1957.

Time marches on - the hours flit by,
And we are travelling - you and I,
In our life's span, we needs must try,
        And pull our weight,
And always aim at something high,
        And no' be late.

Though dreary Winter's wi' us noo,
The Spring will shin be breakin' through!
Keep lukin' oot for something new,
        That's roon the bend,
And wi' a hert that's staunch and true,
        Aye meet a friend.

Oor minister I'm prood tae say,
Has reckoned he maun clim' the brae,
God speed ye aye, and bless your way,
        Whate'er befa',
May licht that never fades, we pray,
        Shine roon your ha'.

And may your work a pleasure be,
Wi' time tae luk aroon and see,
The auld freens, when a day is free,
        Back here at Stair,
And some nicht, maybe bide a wee,
        When you are there.

You're welcome freen, at the but and ben,
Tae play at whist or catch the ten,
You're maybe no' inclined, but then,
        There's lots o' crack,
Tae mak your hair staun up on en',
        We've got the knack.

Or maybe at the curlin' meet,
I ken that's truly up your street,
There's like a shot that's got them beat,
        It is ma son,
While ither broos are wat wi' sweet,
        And have na' won.

But let oor thochts return - it's true,
Oor minister must say adieu,
To your dear wife and children two,
        May God be kind,
Health, wealth and happiness to you,
        And peace of mind.

To Eve and Eddie

Eddie and Eve, a happy pair,
I met them whiles owerby at Stair,
At "Hunterston" they met wi' me,
We chatter ower a cup o' tea.
Nessie and Mrs Connell's cheer,
Is always rich, and guid tae hear,
Nessie comes ben wi' her home bakin',
That just that mornin' she was makin',
Eddie, he'll swiftly wash and dry
The dishes, ere he lays them by.
Richt musical, he's hard tae beat,
He plays the keyboard saft and sweet.
Eve is an expert, I may say,
She names the floors the proper way,
Nae "busy lizzies", - that's too plain,
She ca's them a' their fancy name,
I wish them joy in every way,
Betty and Nessie - add them tae,
This meeting place for you and me,
Where love and freendship holds the key.

Letter from the Clydesdale Bank,

to James Craig Ltd, Auctioneers, Cattle Market, Ayr,
For the attention of the Head Cashier.

Dear Sir,
Ref. - re - Allan Ramsay,
This lad would like to buy some sheep,
Some auld cross ewes, for winter keep,
I would not worry, fret nor fear,
He states he'll pay the head cashier,
You have been done, with quite a few,
But this lad's worth a bob or two!
Should he not pay, - we will decide,
Just hoo tae tak' it oot his hide.

Signed, the Manager of "Hope and Glory",
The Clydesdale Bank in Tobermory.

To Davie Purdie,

Drumjoan, 90th Birthday.

Just give a thought when all alone,
Through ninety years - think of "Drumjoan",
My wish - not special joy and cheer,
Just happy thoughts of yesteryear,
Spend silent hours steeped in the past,
With sweet contentment, till the last.

To Barbara

Written by Marbrack Burn, Sunday July 10th 1960.

Dear Barbara, when the world is still,
Hid from this life of strife and toil,
Beside this mossy mountain rill,
I think of you, at Ardnamoil.

Those days will never more return,
But, oh what "Bliss beyond compare",
(By bracken braes, and babbling burn,)
You had, my child, when you were there.

Though rough would be your parents' road,
For life was hard, and oft-times sore,
They strove, and carried many a load,
And kept at bay, wolf, from the door.

Now time has changed that passing scene,
The steadings now in ruins lie,
Fond memories haunt those pastures green,
A happy place, in days gone by.

As wild fowl haunt the heath clad moor,
As red deer 'mong the mountains roam,
So your dear heart will find the lure,
Of heather hills and valleys, - home.

When I in silence pray for you,
My little maid, I wish you well,
May every blessing, good and true,
Be yours, through life, dear Barbara Bell.

Bed and Breakfast at the Manse at Wick

Dear Friends, I reckon noo and then,
You think whiles o' the Ayrshire men,
Wha cam tae Wick ae nicht at ten,
        By some strange chance,
And were, with pleasure, ushered ben,
        Inside the Manse.

Man, I was glad tae tell ma freens,
O' Scotland's bonnie highland scenes,
O' ladies, we described as queens,
        In hooses sma',
But maist o' a' ma heart aye leans,
        Against you twa.

To think back on the hoose upset,
Twa strangers you had never met,
Arriving like some meteor jet,
        From out the blue,
I cannot understand it yet,
        My friends, can you?

One double bed, and only one,
The Minister, his wife, and son,
Yet they decide what's to be done,
        And this is right,
Believe me folks the lads have won,
        They slept all night.

Though wardrobes met you at the door,
And stuff of all kinds lined the floor,
We thought alone of something more,
        We saw it clear,
The hearts that held the fortress bore,
        True love sincere.

We hope that some day, by and by,
To Ayrshire scenes you'll cast an eye,
And visit here, both Bill and I,
        And sure as fate,
You'll get a bed where you can lie,
        Just fix the date.

Laggan o' Dee

The nearest dwelling to this spot is the Laggan o' Dee,
where we, many times, used to trail, through bog myrtle and peat.

Oor landmark was a green thorn tree,
Beside this shielin' on the Dee,
A welcome warm for you and me,
        I kent braw weil,
That welcome warm, maun aye yet be,
        Within its biel.

The dear auld hoose o' yesteryear,
Gies shelter tae the coo and mere,
The auld herd, - he has wrastled clear,
        Tae his lang hame,
A new hoose biggit unco near,
        Has freens the same.

To Mrs Belford

when she was 96, at a Carsphairn concert.

There's Mrs Belford, my deer freen,
You are the hert o' corn,
It's weil ayont the ninety years,
Since the day that you were born,
God bless you lass, your kin' are scarce,
Their faur apairt and few,
The mair's the pity; Scotland's fame,
Was built wi' folk like you.

To Bob MacTaggart and Adam MacNae

Presentation, 13th April 1966.

The shepherd lads that tend the flock,
Are bred off Scotland's sturdy stock,
This nicht we honour sic a pair,
Here, whaur New Cumnock hauds the fair,
The auldest Herds Fair, truth to tell,
Held in this very Croon Hotel.

There's Bob MacTaggart, kent as Bob,
Been thirty one years in his job,
Each hill he kens for miles aroon',
Each burn and glen beside Loch Doon.

There's Adam, frae Glen Muick, as weil,
A pal o' Bob's, a neighbour chiel,
This nicht we toast, at this great spree,
His years as herd, noo thirty-three,
Mindin' the stock ilk day frae dawn,
At makin' crooks, nae better haun',
Twa lads, weil worthy o' oor praise,
Frae dear auld Scotia's heather braes.

Fill up your glass, hold high the dish,
And listen to my honest wish,
May life throughout be good to you,
In health and wealth, yours ever, Drew.

Written for Drew Hill, 1963.

'Tis July 1963,
We're met in social harmonie,
Tak' in a breath o' freendship here,
And drink a toast tae cronies dear.

For freens indeed I truly hae,
Frae aff Carminnows bonnie brae,
Lang in contentment may ye bide,
Beside your ain dear ingle-side.

I'll min' ye weil, nae doot I ken,
When in some distant but and ben,
These hours I'll cherish all the more,
When wandering on a foreign shore.

Oh I will miss the guid Scotch crack,
Wi' neighbours bidin' at Marbrack,
And long oft-times their joy to share,
And wish and dream that I was there.

For Mr and Mrs Howatson

Waterhead, Drumclog, leaving for New Zealand, Nov. or Dec. 1966.

Ae nicht at Sorn, on the Ayr,
Was held a guid Scotch shepherds' fair,
A couple syne, did beg o' me,
Tae write some lines for ower the sea.

Dear Freens, the scene was joy complete,
Sic cronies frae the hills tae meet,
Frae a' the airts that nicht they came,
A happy team, in freendship's name.

Drumclog hills, steeped in Scottish lore,
You'll mind when on a foreign shore,
And ne'er forget the guid Scotch lays,
O' Ayrshire's bonnie banks and braes.

New Zealand suns, I trust and pray,
Will shine on you for mony a day,
May health and wealth and peace be there,
And love and joy in ample share.

Guidbye dear freens o' Sorn Fair,
I'll aye hae min' I met you there,
I'm sad tae say, oor British law,
Gars a' the best gie faur awa'.

For St Andrew's Nicht

Toastmasters of Ayr, November 1966.

1: Dumfriesshire
There are valleys in Dumfriesshire,
By the Nithsdale heighs and howes,
That in summer suns are paradise complete.
The Maxwelton braes are bonnie,
Grazin' weil contented ewes,
Oh that we could be like them, and never greet.

2: The Borders
This St Andrew's nicht, tae Andrew,
Better kent as cronie Drew,
Man, I'm glad tae be your guest and tarry here;
Tae the land o' bonnie Scotland,

A' these toasts were justly due,
'Tis ma hert that speaks maist honest and sincere.

3:
'Midst the Border land we'll tarry,
By St Mary's Loch sae braw,
By Ettrick and by Teviotdale we'll roam,
In the glory o' the Summer,
Or when smoored wi' Winter's snaw,
To Hogg - the Ettrick Shepherd - this was home.

4: I beong tae Glesca'
I've a hankering aye for Glesca,
Tho' there's aye an unco steer,
And in sic a place I wadna like tae bide,
But there's pride and joy aboot it,
And tae Wull Fyffe it was dear,
Especially the ship yairds o' the Clyde.

5: Auld Reekie
Now tae Scotland's fairest city,
We'll return and bide a wee,
And we'll walk the Royal Mile when dawn is grey,
Ere the hurrying feet o' travellers,
Oot tae win an honest fee,
Stir the silence o' the scene, at break of day.

6:
See the rock and misty castle,
And the gardens steeped in dew,
Sir Walter Scott - his monument sublime,
'Tis a thrill to be a Scotsman,
When these wondrous works you view,
Or in honours name to gaze upon the shrine.

7: Ayrshire
Whaur bonnie Doon rins wimplin',
First licht o' day I saw,
Ae December in a hamely but an' ben,
Twa or three miles frae the cottage,
Whaur, midst Jan'war's sleet and snaw,
Was born, the pride o'. Ayrshire's famous men.

8:
For frae every neuk and crannie,
O' the lands across the sea,
There are herts that dearly lo'e oor Scottish lore,
Sae be prood my freens o' Scotland,
And your Ayrshire pedigree,
Tho' you wander to a distant foreign shore.

9: Bonnie Gallowa'
Oh to stray doon in the Glenkens,
Viewing Corserine and Craignaw,
By the Carlin's Cairn, and by the Loch o' Dee,
There. the muse is like the mountains,
O' this Bonnie Gallowa',
For the mind, it is inspired thro' een that see.

10:
Oh to wake up at the dawning,
And to hear the skylark's lay,
As on wings he trills his music to the skies,
Or at sundown scan the shieling,
On the lonely heather brae,
It is joy to see the peat reek rise.

11: Fareweil
When the pairtin' oor has chappit,
And we a' maun tak' the gait,
May the shepherd lead us safely tae oor bield,
And, like Milton, we'll be lichtsome,
Though we only watch and wait,
Till we meet anither nicht, - a fond fareweil.

For Bill Paterson at Coylton Re-union

January 1967.

The auld schule, whaur in years lang gane,
Gaed mony a feart and backward wean,
And yet, where some intent to climb,
Aspired to heights and works sublime;
And some, though plodders through and through,
Their hert was warm, and always true;
And some in foreign realms sojourn,
And some are gane, - they'll ne'er return.
The auld schule means tae me and mine,
Dear happy days o' auld langsyne,

But progress maun be sair hame pressed,
A new schule's built, - may it be blessed,
And may oor weans high hopes fulfill,
Wha's sail was set, at Culton schule

Lines to Mr William MacGeoch

on his retiral as car park attendant at Castle Douglas mart.

On Market Hill we'll miss ye sair,
I ettled aye tae see ye there,
Each time I cam' tae special fair,
    You welcomed me,
You gar'd me set my motor square,
    Syne pey ma fee.

Dear Willie, - man I'll miss yer crack,
A couthie tongue, ye didna' lack,
A smile that only chiels can mak',
    That hae your wit,
At parkin' caurs, you had the knack,
    Dead on the bit.

I've been in mony Scottish toons,
And met wi' freendly canty loons,
But never Wull, in a' ma roons,
    Did ere I meet,
A callant that could pit caurs doon,
    Sae straught and neat.

Fu' mony times I've seen me grin,
At great caur parks, - you're aye shut in,
They're shoutin' numbers, "Shift this yin,
    Let Sanny oot."
At Castle Douglas, yes you win,
    Without a doot.

Sae lad, I wish ye lots o' cheer,
Good health and joy for mony a year,
And whiles your shanks you'll maybe steer,
    Tae Wallet's Mairt,
Whaur a' yer cronies, maist sincere,
    Will warm yer hert.

The Clachan o' Dalry

Fu' mony years we've daunered roon,
Among the Glenkens braes,
Amid the joys o' Summer suns,
We've spent some happy days.
The greatest things in life are free,
What gowd can never buy,
Like freens aroon the Glenkens,
And the Clachan o' Dalry.

Tae hike oot ower the heath clad muir,
Far frae the noise and steer,
Tae hear the skylarks trembly lays,
Sweet music to the ear,
Tae see the sunset's golden ball,
Like flame bedeck the sky,
You'll see it frae your ain wee hoose,
In the Clachan o' Dalry.

The shrill note o' the lang nebbed whaup,
Throughoot the mosshags ring,
The peeweep whiles will screch and scream,
On flichtsome flappin' wing.
The moorhen frae the lochan bank,
Will scoot, withoot a cry,
A mere stane throw frae whaur ye bide,
In the Clachan o' Dalry.

Add tae these thrills the rod and line,
And I am borne away,
To where in wintry forenichts lang,
My thochts are apt tae stray,
To where, when simmer days are braw,
The gentle art I try,
Tae lure the speckled troot, - I'm keen,
For miles aroon Dalry.

To wade by lochs o' silver sand,
Is ever dear tae me,
Tae watch the ring, - a risin' fish,
And syne tae cast the flee.
Next mornin' hoo we smack oor lips,
When bonny troots we fry,
Faur better than the fishman sells,
In the Clachan o' Dalry.

Noo, tae the folks, I'm bound tae turn,
Wi' herts as true as steel,
Some that I kent are gane lang syne,
Woodhead and lonely Shiel;
But generations new maun rise,
Tae herd, and milk the kye,
And come on Sunday tae the kirk,
In the Clachan o' Dalry.

Tae crack beside the ingle neuk,
When nichts are dour and snell,
The glow inside warms ilka hert,
The peat reek warms oorsel',
Sic nichts like this when cronies meet,
Nae chiel should ask me why,
I'm happy here, in this wee toon,
The Clachan o' Dalry.

Dear freens, wha bide in this braw place,
And freens frae faur awa,
Be prood o' this bit Scottish soil,
In Bonnie Gallowa',
Whaur martyrs names enrich the scroll,
On history's page, gane by,
God bless, - in faith, and hope, and love,
In St John's Toon o' Dalry.

The Rodden Tree

Told to Jim and I by Cameron Thomson, horn-carver, Lawers Toll, Aberfeldy, 6th April 1967.

I heeded what you said to me,
"Just snip a bit o' rodden tree,
Within the boat, there let it be,
        And quietly wait,
A salmon's shair tae hae a pree,
        And grup yer bait."

Sae free', when licht cam' ower the brae,
I daunered, at the screch o' day,
Among the trees that clad Loch Tay,
        Though bare o' green,
I spied a braw young rodden, say,
        A twig, nipped clean.

I placed it whaur ma e'e could spy,
Richt in the boat wi' Jim and I,
We set the lures, - the oars we ply,
        Oor day's begun,
Bang goes the reel, he's on, man aye,
        Hale sixteen pun'.

I'll ne'er forget that simple tale,
When a' loch fishers fancies fail,
You plod awa' through sleet and gale,
        And nothing see,
But I'll hae min', before I sail,
        The rodden tree.

To Willie Thomson on leaving "Springs"

May 1967.

Dear Friend, I feel the changing scene,
May touch the heart strings, at the core,
Ne'er let the phrase, - "What might have been",
O'er rule the quest, - "What lies before".
"The best in life is yet to be",
Great words, the Prophet ever sings,
Take with you, friend, the Golden Key,
That never closed the door at Springs.

Greetings

Dear Friends, might I today express,
Best wishes for your happiness,
Health is the world's most precious bliss,
May God be kind, and give you this.
Here also, I would ask and pray,
For peace of mind, from day to day,
Then, it is yours to give and take,
The love, that homes, not mansions, make,
Such gifts, so good, and keenly sought,
Are not with gold and silver bought,
These wishes true, penned on this card,
Are sign, sincere, "The Ayrshire Bard",
                                Allan Ramsay.

Carsphairn in Galloway

I have wandered oft times in the Highlands,
By Helmsdale, and Thurso, and Wick,
I've strayed many miles,
In the far Western Isles,
Wi' the cromach, - the old hazel stick.
I have made many friends on my travels,
And I trust many more I may meet,
But I tell you right here,
With a heart that's sincere,
That Galloway's gie ill tae beat.

I have tarried at times by Fort William,
And gazed at the mountains and bens,
I have sauntered for days,
By the Glenfinnan braes,
And marvelled at gullies and bens.
In Skye I have wound by the Coolins,
And spent happy hours in Portree,
But the hert that beats true,
Has a longing for you,
For Galloway's dearest tae me.

Inspiring is Lewis and Harris,
Wi' grey rugged rocks a' aroon,
The crofters ower there,
Hae aye time tae spare,
Tae forgether in Stornoway toon.
They were diggin' the peat in the mairland,
And biggin' them neat in the stack,
There was peace and content,
Wherever I went,
But Galloway beckons me back.

I have viewed the great glory o' London,
And traversed the throng busy street,
The Westminster Halls,
And mighty St Paul's,
With the echo of hurrying feet.
But where is the calm in the city?
I sigh for the mountain and plain,
Where the heather clad knowes,
Breed the the herd and the ewes,
Grey Galloway, - this is oor ain.

Even sailed on the great Indian Ocean,
Thro' South African cities I've strolled,
    In the broad Durban Street,
    There the Mayor I did meet,
And in friendship his tale to me told.
With the wee darkie lads I was happy,
In all that I heard and I saw,
    But my heart strings are set,
    In the old country yet,
Mang the mountains o' auld Gallowa'.

I have viewed the braw lakes o' Killarney,
In Dublin's fair city I've been,
    To auld Donegal,
    I have answered the call,
Where the shamrock is shining and green.
But the lure o' the magnet is steady,
And the cry o' the whaup I pursue,
    I'll come back to Marbrack,
    At the end o' the track,
At the end o' the road, back to you.

This nicht is a great social meeting,
O' braw lads and lassies I ken,
    There are staunch herts and true,
    Frae the valleys I lo'e,
Real ladies and fine gentlemen.
When the main spring gets weary and wabbit,
And the blind is pu'd doon ower my e'e,
    Where the Jordan runs slow,
    I will cross the Great Flo',
And ca' it, - "The Water o' Dee."

Poem

When ower the hin'maist sheugh we slide,
And sprachle tae the tither side,
The Maister's book is open wide,
        He'll read oor name,
And tally up, and sin' decide,
        Wha's played the game.

He'll speir, although He's bound tae ken,
Just hoo we lo'ed oor fellow men,
And, did we offer, noo and then,

Tae egg them on,
And, if we did, He'll say come ben,
And gie's yer haun.

But, if o' life we've made a hash,
And worshipped only gowd and cash,
He'll tell us noo, we neednа' fash,
We'll wear nae croon,
O' sic like folk His hauns He'll wash,
And turn them doon.

To Revd. John Good of Twynholm

being requested to preach at Crathie Kirk on Sunday 17th September 1967 by the Queen and Royal Family.

That wee bit news I read yestreen,
Gar'd my pen write tae you auld freen,
Tae preach at Crathie tae oor Queen,
You'll fit the part,
There, on a Sabbath morn serene,
Inspire the heart.

To Aileen and Colin Hope

on their Wedding 24th July 1968.

The year is Nineteen Sixty-Eight,
And Twenty-Fourth July, the date,
This day dear Aileen's won her claim,
She's changed her life, and changed her name.

In Faith, you have been woo'd and won,
In love this union is begun,
Now surely Aileen you will cope,
With Faith and Love, as Mrs. Hope.

Now Colin, teach her day by day,
To clean and cook the proper way,
Best wishes to you both, and try,
To add a "Little Hope" forby.

Signed Jim and Liz, uncle and aunt,
Frae that wee place ca'ed Minishant.

To Mr. Muirhead

With the gift of a Scottish porridge bowl and horn spoon, July 1968.

The halesome parritch, chief o' Scotia's flood,
The bowl and spoon o' generations gane,
The toil worn cottar, in his day was prood,
Tae sup the richt guid fare, and envy nane.

There, on a white scrubbed dresser, by the wa',
Are rows o' bowls wi' patterned plates combined,
An Ayrshire, hamely cot, what scene sae braw,
The cottage leaves the palace far behind.

Mrs Marr

Died 1st August 1968.

Dear Lord, and Captain, of the craft we steer,
Whose guiding light has led us year by year,
Be very near and comfort us this day,
And send thy peace, and bless us Lord, we pray.

Our mortal frame, prone to life's ills, doth rust,
And, at the last, returns thy dust to dust,
But we, (through faith), of death can have no fear,
The soul doth enter an eternal sphere.

By woodlands green, high water mark, Loch Tay,
Here, in the haven of Ardeonaig bay,
This dust we leave, close by the aged pier,
Thus, we fulfil the wish of one held dear.

Return us Lord, in safety, this we ask,
Each to his own appointed earthly task,
Only the best will count when we complete,
Our final figures on God's balance sheet.
Grant grace, and mercy, and Thy peace divine,
Dwell in our hearts, - the glory, Lord, is thine.

Birthdays

It was a thrill, when, as a child, we had a birthday treat,
But now that we are older grown we'd rather not compete,
The prize is not for wha's had most, the number counts the same,
The marks are for, what deeds are done, and how we played the game.

The Moat Toll Smiddy

When I was just a chiel at schule,
It used tae be a joy,
Tae staun' beside the smiddy fire,
It thrilled me when a boy,
Tae watch the flying spark that flew,
Like fireworks through the door,
Tae smell the burning horses hoofs,
Tae hear the bellows roar,
The anvil's clang was music sweet,
Eachtime we ventured in,
Tae see the red hot iron take shape,
For horses must ha'e shin,
The Clydesdales stood for 'oors on en',
Work horse o' high degree,
Frae fermers, and contractors baith,
For miles roon Ochiltree.
This scene, alas, is gone for good,
Ceased, is the bellows roar,
The iron doth rust, the wood doth rot,
The smiddy is no more,
Though there are many scenes like this,
Remembered on life's scroll,
My heart is wae for one I loved,
Kent as the "Old Moat Toll",
Oor handy smiths, the Burton boys,
Willie and John were there,
And Tam and Nan, I'll no lee oot,
A foursome, fair and square,
The auld stane wa's are noo in stoor,
Like men, they too decay,
As long's I leeve I'll ne'er forget,
The smiddy on the brae.

What Doth it Profit a Man

He said he had a lot in life,
In great possessions valued high,
A mansion house with fittings fine,
The best that gold could ever buy,
He held deed titles of the land,
The choicest fields in fertile range,
He made good profits through the years,
By dealings in the stock exchange,
His barns with harvest grain were full,
He'd have to sell the overflow,
If market trends were slightly flat,
He'd hold, because the price was low,
His flock, his herd, was pedigreed,
All chosen from some noted strain,
And he himself, Ah! proud was he,
The common man he did disdain,
He did not say, "Good morning, Friend",
Because his friends were very few,
He did not give away a smile,
Compassion's tear, he never knew,
No song had he within his hear,
No sympathy or tender care,
And when he died the world moved on,
Death duty claimed the lion's share,
His gold, his jewels, stock and land,
Were sliced with earth's steel hardened knife,
He missed the joy, the peace, the friends,
The crown of love, in human life.

Last's Not Always Least

Aft times we feel the die is cast,
Against us in life's station,
E'en though my freen ye're drawn the last,
Ye mauna heid frustration,
The last at times the first can be,
The lowest, whiles the greatest,
I've seen the biggest michty wee,
The earliest whiles the latest.

Wedding Wishes

Ah, wedding bells in early spring,
A golden band - a wedding ring,
My wishes are sincere and true,
To bride Maureen, and Bridegroom Drew,
May health, and peace, and love reign high,
Earth's greatest gifts gold cannot buy,
God bless and keep you night and day,
Your constant family friend - J.K.

Written to Jim Drennan

on his wedding in Australia.

Love's old sweet song claims heart and hand,
Far frae the shores o' Scotia's land,
But Ayrshire's freenship mauna' break,
And sae we sen' for auld time's sake,
The best o' wishes warm and true,
Tae this dear lass, Jim, and tae you,
Health, peace, and joy, earth's greatest bliss,
And love, the crown of happiness,
Shut ticht yer een, and you will see,
Ma haun' held oot across the sea.

Valentine

Oh darling I am sad at heart,
I weep the whole day through,
I long to hold and never part,
With you, and only you.

Please come to me and hold me tight,
And say you will be mine,
And I will cuddle you each night,
My darling Valentine.

Ballochbeatties Fishing Lodge

Dear friend, I ask what brought you here,
To such a silence and retreat,
You seek perchance a lower gear,
Or shelter from the throng-filled street.

Or in some office block upstair,
You're held between grim walls of stone,
You simply crave the clearer air,
Of hills and valleys, lost and lone.

I say relax, breathe full and deep,
And eat fresh trout, lured by the fly,
And rest in undisturbed sleep,
Till whaups and oyster catchers cry.

Recawr, Macatterick's, gentle art,
With fishing rods and casts and line,
The thrill that fills your inward heart,
Has oft times cheered and strengthened mine.

A rising trout, a Teal and Green,
A Wickham's Fancy on the tail,
Anticipation holds the scene,
As round the island rocks we sail.

As coot and mallard haunt the reeds,
To feed by shallows, lined in sedge,
Or slimy shores where water weeds,
Are washed around the peaty edge.

Likewise we dine by sheltered nook,
On hamely fare, in full supply,
(Packed by a grand experienced cook),
Now spread beneath an open sky.

No peace in all the world can be,
Like silent hours 'mong hill and glen,
No mind relaxing dream so free,
Far from the files of desk or pen.

When evening shadows fade and fail,
To Ballochbeatties Lodge we ply,
We'll list' to many a fishers tale,
While nation's news we all pass by.

Old faithful friends of yesteryear,
Stole care free hours from worldly strife,
These signatures, though fading here,
Are shining in the Book of Life.

Dear Ballochbeatties, cast this line,
Where every note is sweet and pure,
Long may each fisher friend o' mine,
Be spared to tread this heather moor.

If in Life

If in life we fight the battle,
With a heart that's staunch and true,
If we shoulder high the burden that we bear,
If we love sincere our neighbour,
We can see the struggle through,
If the game we play is always fair and square.

If we jog along the highway,
And no matter whom we meet,
If we hail them with a smile and say "Hello",
We will raise the hopes when dreary,
Of a comrade in the street,
Then the light of love we shed, we'll never know.

If we wave to every cronie,
We will never feel alone,
Do not grudge a little comfort at the call,
You will hear an inward singing,
From a heart that is your own,
And you'll find a peace when evening shadows fall.

We are treading paths of glory,
Where the sun will surely shine,
Where the peace and joy are boundless as the sea,
We will pray that such a bonus,
Will be labelled yours and mine,
When at last we must return the Golden Key.

At the Wedding of Douglas and Teena

July 17th 1970.

Back in September 'Sixty Eight,
A wee lad cam' tae oor croft gate,
Seekin' a shelter frae the win',
Wi' bite and sup of coorse flung in.
We thocht we micht gie him a try,
And Douglas said, "Och aye, och aye",
"Whit is your job?" I had tae speir,
"An agricultural engineer."
Well Douglas did his job and he,
Got roon aboot in his MG,
Till Teena Grant, oor bride today,
Fixed Douglas, I am bound tae say,
Being a nurse, his pulse did check,
And fixed a bandage roon his neck,
His MG then he had to ban,
And swapped it for a Mini van,
May all the sores in life's highway,
Be scratches you can kiss away,
And all the hurts that come to you,
Be healed by love's refreshing dew,
May joy and peace in ample share,
Shine aye aroon' oor happy pair,
Long spared in health - in love held fast,
Along life's road from first to last,
Signed, - by the Wypers, at their base,
Plus, a' the dugs aboot the place.

Reply to Sam Hay

Tarbolton, for 20th October 1970.

Dear Sam, my boy, I had your note,
And (mind ye son), I get a lot,
But since Tarbowton is the toon,
I canna turn yer letter doon,
Lang syne I leeved in it masel',
I've heard the bellman ring the bell,
Ma mither ta'en me roon Hood's Hill,
Doon tae the Fail at Willie's Mill,
Och aye, I'll come on that date freen',
Afore ye start yer Halloween,
That nicht ma yarns, tae ane an' a',

Will be o' Bonnie Gallowa',
I hope I'll be in richt guid fettle,
That's whit Tarbowton folks'll ettle,
I'll drap in by, if I am sober,
Afore the twentieth o' October,
Tae see if plans are workin' richt,
And sae, ma freen', I'll say "Guidnicht".

To Drew Stevenson

October 1970.

Congratulations, my dear freen,
Your name was in the "Post" yestreen,
You'll lo'e the herts o' ane and a',
And coup the stanes o' Hadrian's Wa'.

The water o' the Mersey tide,
You'll poor oot ower the Scottish Clyde,
That's what we twa, baith, fain wad see,
And pray that men micht brithers be.

Best wishes frae a hert that's true,
I send, in freendship's name, tae you,
We'll talk things ower next time we rove,
Doon by Lairdmannoch's treasure trove.

To J. Kerr

Leicester.

So now our lines are clean and dry,
Our rods, our reels, are all laid by,
I trust these reels again will sing,
At Loch Tay, in the early Spring,
May your reel to perfection run,
Oft-times, my friend, in Seventy-One.

Keep Britain Tidy

Never throw your car'mel papers,
Out into the open road,
Such untidy careless capers,
Stressed should be in "Highway Code".

Britain must show tidy habits,
Litter never seen or found,
Be like common country rabbits,
Hide your "litter" underground.

The River Doon

Sent with a book of the above title, to Thomas Muirhead, in Victoria, Christmas 1970.

Sit doon my freen, and trusty cronie,
And read o' Doon, wha's braes are bonnie,
Start wi' the hills o' Gallowa',
Whaur a' Doon's headland waters fa',
Smell the bog myrtle, by the flo',
And pu' some heather, as you go.
Come through Ness Glen, beside the stream,
And dauner on, as in a dream,
Until Kirk Alloway comes near,
A spot tae you that aye was dear,
The Doonfoot shore, - the open sea,
Nocht else divides Tam, - you and me.

New Year Wishes

Although the scene is cold I choose,
And the gate is closed you view,
These wishes sent are glowing warm,
And the gate is open too.

May every blessing fill your hearts,
Along the track you steer,
And may the Ardeonaig sport be good,
Dear freens, - A Guid New Year.

Golden Wedding Wishes

My dear lo'ed freens frae Newtonmore,
A wee bird cam tae oor ha' door,
And whistled in my listening ear,
Your Golden Wedding was this year.

Again you'll hear the wedding bells,
May health and joy bide wi' yersels,
That's fifty years you've been thegither,
God grant ye mair wi' yin anither.

These wishes sent tae Newtonmore,
Are frae yer freens at High Pinmore.

Toast

I trust this nicht your joy will be,
In fullest measure, richt and free,
May a' herts there ring oot wi' glee,
        And a' combine,
Tae add in freendship - harmonie,
        For auld lang syne.

To Mr & Mrs Galloway

Balmaclellan, on their Golden Wedding, March 12th 1971.

In early spring o' 'twenty-one,
The blackbird sang his lay,
The mavis joined the morning choir,
A stirring roundelay.

The year is Nineteen Seventy-One,
That's fifty years sin' syne,
It is a Golden Wedding day,
And still the sun can shine.

The songsters still can trill the air,
Taught by "The Master's Voice",
We'll join with them and say to you,
In such blest peace - rejoice.

A Wedding Wish

For Mrs Dean.

Ring wedding bells on this glad day,
For Maureen, strike a joyful strain;
For John, a tender love song play,
And blend the two in sweet refrain,
May all the best that's yet to be,
Outshine the best that's ever been,
Cherished in love's eternal key,
From your well-wisher, Mrs Dean.

Spring

Little birds are singing sweetly,
Little flowers begin to peep,
They have wakened after Winter,
From their long and dreary sleep.

Birds come back from other countries,
That have been away so long,
Now they try to make us cheery,
Singing such a lively song.

Little robins are so happy,
That they whistle and they sing,
Everybody feels so joyful,
For they know that this is Spring.

The Lost Hat

[Allan Ramsay's first poem, written at the age of six]

One day as I was standing upon a stack of hay,
There came an awful gust of wind, and blew my hat away.

I chased it for about a mile, but what was worse than ever,
I was just going to pick it up when it blew into the river.

At last it came into the side and then I got a hold,
But when I saw it in my hand it was something to behold.

When I got home the first I met it was my little brother,
Says he to me, says I to him, "I'll have to buy another."

Out Motoring

We started on a Winter's day,
Big Jock and I together,
The wind, it was a little cold,
But not the worst of weather.

'Twas in the motor that we went,
With henhouses on board,
Jock only took one pint in Ayr,
That's all he could afford.

'Twas Girvan we were making for,
Crosshill we had to pass,
His thoughts were of a public house,
And of another glass.

When through Crosshill we rumbled on,
No other pub preventing,
Although within myself I knew,
That he was left lamenting.

Our destination soon was reached,
We soon were homeward set,
But all the way to Minishant,
A pint he did not get.

As all the others on the way,
Were closed, this was the first,
And by the time we reached that same,
He almost died from thirst.

Now cheerier still we moved along,
Without the least sensation,
Till something made us stop in style,
Which caused a consternation.

This point, my friends, I now will tell,
Although against my will,
Into a newfilled drain we went,
At the gates to Castlehill.

"By crimes," said Jock. "We're in a hole,"
This he saith unto me,
And unto him I answered thus,
"Yes, sir, we seem to be."

A motor lorry then was got,
To pull us from the drain,
But all the pulling it could pull,
Alas! was proved in vain.

A motor crane came past that way,
Which quickly raised us out,
Yet when they placed it there at first,
We were inclined to doubt.

We borrowed lights to keep us right,
And make us quite secure,
But ere Jock left the town that night,
His life he did insure.

And now that we are safely home,
Says I, "Let's say no more."
Yet on that very night I'm sure,
He told about a score.

"To be a sober man," says he,
"And drive into a dyke,
It's more than I can understand,
I've never heard the like."

And that is all I've got to say,
Before I say "Adieu,"
"Beware of those who don't drink (and drive),
As well as those who do."

Time

How swift the hours go rolling past,
The days and years, they follow fast,
Man lives his life 'midst joys and woes,
Until he earns his long repose.

While in the grave he quietly rests,
His name is read by passing quests,
Upon a stone it's chiselled clear,
That it may stand for many a year.

Alas! 'tis like unto a flower,
That grows with others on the bower,
Soon it will wither and be gone,
And shall no more be looked upon.

Our names, just now, are clear as day,
As time moves on they will decay,
Till soon from off our earthly stone,
They're swallowed in oblivion.

A Family Affair

I'll start my rhyme with Jock himself,
A man of stature tall,
He loves his wife, and daughters too,
But Whitletts best of all.

When disagreeing with your word,
He thinks you are not true,
Just slip a bob into his hand,
And he will swear by you.

Last New Year's Day he went to shoot,
Some cartridges he bought,
And though the hares lay side by side,
He never fired a shot.

For reasons why he never fired,
I've tried to find a clue,
But now, at last, I am convinced,
He is a blinking Jew!

Then Mrs Robson, head of all,
Is busy all the while,
With keeping all the others right,
A constant job in style.

She always sees them off to work,
With smiles upon their faces,
She has to watch them, or they might
Forget to tie their laces.

The minister, he sometimes calls,
It's always pretty late,
He sits for hours, and then departs,
He does not like to wait.

Whene'er they hear a knock at night,
At least I've heard it said,
That half the people in the house,
Go tumbling into bed.

But Mrs Robson's worst of all,
For when the parson's gone,
She dreamily gets out of bed,
With shoes and stockings on.

There's Mary, but she keeps things quiet,
She's wise, then none can tell,
No good or bad I know of her,
It's maybe just as well.

Then Janet, she is extra good,
At dreaming in the night,
I heard of this some days ago,
And know that it is right.

The bus in which she travels home,
Is very often busy,
She usually has to stand,
Perhaps it makes her dizzy.

So this is what she dreams about,
When she is in her bed,
"I'll bring the bus right to the mill,
To where I work," she said.

But she is good at something else,
Expert, without a doubt,
On paper this must not be seen,
So I will leave it out.

Now Mirn, I'm doing this on chance,
But I will have a go,
I think I'm running quite a risk,
But still you never know.

Just now she works' in Gilchrist's shop,
A bakers in the town,
She packs the cookies for the vans,
But does it upside down.

Right in a cellar under-ground,
Without a scrap of bedding,
She shuts a man the whole night through,
The night before his wedding.

Then on her birthday she receives,
A cake, all nicely made,
But it turns out to be a tin,
On which the icing's laid.

I'm wondering now just what to say,
I think I'll let it be,
Whatever happens now I know,
There's something in for me.

Love Sick

Alas! there's something wrong with me,
I'm thinner every day,
The doctor says if this goes on,
I'll jolly soon decay,
He does not give me medicine,
He knows it would not do,
It's all for want of you, Mary,
It's all for want of you.

So hurry up and cure yourself,
For I am in a plight,
I cannot work throughout the day,
I cannot sleep at night,
I never eat between the meals,
I'm turning like a slate,
Oh that I only knew the worst,
But I shall have to wait.

I see you sitting by the fire,
And yet you're never warm,
Your bound to be a nuisance too,
(I don't mean any harm),
And if you think it's harm I mean,
My words I must restrain,
To sort the clothes I will proceed,
And close my eyes again.

I'm sitting upright in my bed,
The clothes are in a heap,
It's slightly after twelve o'clock,
And I am not asleep,
The fault you say's entirely mine,
But wherefore is it due,
It's all because of you, Mary,
It's all because of you.

This Scent was Sent costing four Cents.

This scent is scent you ought to like,
'Tis sent from one you know,
I might have sent you something else,
But scent is all the go.

This scent should just be used in drops,
This scent is worth the money,
This scent is scent sent through the post,
To you my dearest honey.

Perhaps you don't like scent at all,
But this is sent on trial,
Just think of him who sent this scent,
And don't screw up your dial.

Still if you are dissatisfied,
Just send it back to me,
And I will send it back to where,
I got the guarantee.

In Paradise

Listen! I want you dear,
Someone has sent me here,
Someone I want to clear,
        So far protected.
You were among the flock,
That night at ten o'clock,
Don't look as dense as rock,
        You are connected.

No names I mean to name,
Lest I get into blame,
Home in the bus they came,
        Full of their capers.
One chap who had to stand,
Seemed to be in the band,
Got sweets from girl's own hand,
        Wrapped up in papers.

Soft hat on man nearby,
Holds fast the fellow's eye,
Some girls are in the pie,
        Will there be ruction?
Papers in hat are laid,
Not a remark is made,
Many a grin is stayed,
        After the action.

One lady, almost gray,
Not in the pie, I'll say,
Sees papers right away,
        What is she saying?
She and the gent confide,
Chap looks from side to side,
Nowhere around to hide,
        Watch him, he's praying!

Still stands his body whole,
Off, he has reached the Toll,
After him come a shoal,
        All of them "Misses",
No stars are in the skies,
No moon has dared to rise,
Seems like a paradise,
        Acting in kisses XXX.

Girls to the right of him,
Girls to the left of him,
Girls are in front of him,
        Heavens! he cosy.
Surely he's managed well,
Keep quiet and do not tell,
Hide this from those who smell,
        Rats, and get nosey.

Tell it not unto Gath, lest he gets smitten,
Askelon must not hear, thus it is written.
This writer should beware,
Choosing his words with care,
Having a fearless air,
        Innocent tender.
Whom does he write about?
Himself the people doubt,
Dash it! The truth is out,
        I'm the offender.

A Mournful Tale

Sad is the tale I'm writing now,
Each knee should bend, each head should bow,
It happened, but I don't know how,
        I've asked in vain.
A certain man, if he'll allow,
        I will explain.

This man in question, what is he,
A sawyer of the first degree,
He can't be truly called T.T.
        That's rather plain,
In fact there's times he seems to be,
        Just hardly sane.

Of him alone I mean to write,
That means no sleep for me tonight,
One day, that is in broad day light,
        He comes to grief,
Two fingers vanish from his sight,
        A pound of beef.

His daughters thought his heart would fail,
So each one bought a mourning veil,
In hospital I heard him wail,
        But he was faking,
The place for him was in the jail,
        And no mistaking.

Whene'er it happened I can swear,
He made the whisky disappear,
It helped his downward hopes to cheer,
        He's struggled through,
And lives to drink his pint of beer,
        Or maybe two.

A Doctor's Verdict

Big Jock took ill one winter morn,
'Twas just about the dawn,
His face was white as any sheet,
I've ever looked upon.

I got him home with much ado,
I nearly had a spill,
The people cried, "He's kidding you,
He means to have a GILL."

Jock always shouted of the pain,
Says he, "It's really trying."
Says I, "My lad I doubt," says I,
"Your only cure is dying."

Soon Doctor K was called upon,
And came to see the fellow.
Says Jock, "Oh boys, my pains are bad,"
Says K, "So is your bellow."

The doctor told the trouble quick,
He says, "It's most emphatic,
The fact of the matter is," says he,
"You are a pure lunatic."

If a battering is forthcoming, the last line reads:
"Your trouble is rheumatic."

A Cheery Sunday Evening

Oh heavens! here's a rummy go,
An incident that all should know,
I'll write it plain the world may see,
The blame, of course, will fall on me,
But I will risk it yet once more,
I've been in trouble oft before,
The entertainment was a treat,
In fact, it would be hard to beat.

This stunt occurred one Sunday night,
I know the actors just by sight,
All told, they only numbered three,
A man, and wife, who can't agree,
Their daughter must be in the pie,
Although she is a trifle shy,
But here she is the heroine,
The act began at five past nine.

The boss arises from his chair,
He lifts the pen with thorough care,
The ink is finished, that's a spite,
To me it was a great delight.
He sends the daughter off to borrow,
She states she'll send it back tomorrow.
A bottle, rimming to the brim,
She boldy hands across to him.

When all his writing was complete,
He grasped the bottle rather neat,
He thought his daughter had a hold,
The words he used can not be told,
His fine grey jacket, almost new,
Was coloured to the elbows, blue,
But look behind, forbear to mock,
Behold it is a speckled frock.

Her nice clean stockings, what a shame,
But who the devil is to blame,
The lady of the house buts in,
Oh hurry up and see who'll win.
She has to take the daughter's part,
In case the darling breaks her heart,
At this the man gets worse than ever,
He made the very walls to shiver.

The girl was glad to get away,
The ink she's surely bound to pay,
She took right back the empty dish,
Good luck to her I had to wish,
She sketched the woman out a tale,
And one she's sketched can never fail,
Back home she comes the storm still rages,
Like heathens in the middle ages.

To keep the mother on her side,
(For that alone would save her hide,)
She starts to wash the dishes up,
But through excitement breaks a cup,
The father might have gone his mile,
But thought it hardly worth his while,
Thus, things were normal now, once more,
As they had been an hour before.

But every night it is the same,
No matter whence or how you came,
They'll give you tea, without a doubt,
But watch till you are safely out,
One night, the milk was sour, I got,
"Put plenty in, the tea is hot,"
They calmly say, we didn't know,
Take my advice, and DO NOT GO.

A Midnight Stroll

The world is hushed, the air is still,
Quiet is the vale, and quiet the hill,
A softer night I've never seen,
And more tired I have never been.

It happened not so long ago,
The tale perhaps you do not know,
But those who knew upon that night,
Their temperatures were out of sight.

John Ross, that was the fellow's name,
Along with me that day he came,
Our bicycles we both got ready,
Says John, "My tyres are true and steady."

A Sunday afternoon was this,
That is a part I must not miss,
To Monkwood Mains we took the road,
About ten meiles from our abode.

Arriving there within the hour,
We wandered out to have a tour,
And, to the church we lastly went,
Although we were not really sent.

That night the singing sounded great,
The usual being second rate,
The bass, it made a few look round,
So incomparable was the sound.

We had our tea when church was o'er,
And on the road we were once more,
We had no lights, the bridge we're at,
John's steady tyre goes steady flat.

With keys and patches, at the double,
We very soon were out of trouble,
But, ere we'd gone quite half a mile,
A mighty crack we heard in style.

No words can tell, no term will fit,
I'll merely say the tyre was split,
Says John, "I'll ride your bike, that's fine,
You'll sit behind and steady mine."

The plan was quickly put in force,
Says he, "It's simple, brains of course."
Till at the hedge he looked enticed,
And in the ditch the lot capsized.

This is the cause of brains, thinks I,
As in among the wheels we lie,
Although, 'twas sure a great invention,
To walk, was now our proved intention.

I walked with John, right into Ayr,
And then, I cycled home from there,
When at the gate I saw a croud,
"Is that you?" someone cried aloud.

I said it was, in my best tones,
With fear and trembling in my bones,
"John will be marching onward yet,"
And all the rest I did relate.

Next day, my pal seemed fairly cheery,
But still, he looked a little weary,
'Twas vaseline he was out to seek,
To ease his tired and blistered feet.

And oft since then I've seen the fun,
And thought on ways I might have done;
When thinking, months long past the scene,
We think on things that might have been.

When the Polis blows his whistle

Perhaps you'll think it rather strange,
I've chosen such a theme,
The truth I'll tell in every line,
I don't recall a dream.
Now everyone has been in town,
When Summer suns have shone,
And you've heard the polis whistle,
But marched indignant on.

One night in Ayr, I mind it well,
I saw a splendid show,
A piece of stuff, (but what is that?
A lady, don't you know.)
Was walking, boldly, on the road,
(A road I've often gone,)
When the polis blew his whistle,
But she marched indignant on.

The sound was really meant for her,
Because she'd dropped her belt,
The thing had just been hanging loose,
And slipped away unfelt,
Of course, she dare not turn about,
In case the crowd made fun,
Though again he blew his whistle,
She marched indignant on.

Now cast your eyes a little space,
Upon the man in blue,
His lips are forming sweary words,
And more than one or two,
He gathers all the wind he has,
The very earth he shook,
She squints at first, there's something wrong,
She condescends to look.

Her face gets scarlet right away,
For when she looked he signed,
The belt was lying on the road,
Perhaps a mile behind,
Her only hope was walking back,
And that was now begun,
For now, she wished, she'd looked at first,
Instead of marching on.

Now here's advice to everyone,
When walking on the street,
You never ought to mind the skies,
Or gaze upon your feet,
But, mind the sounds you hear around,
Before your face gets red,
When you hear the polis whistle,
For God's sake, raise your head.

The Shrine

(Edinburgh)

A day to be remembered this has been,
A day that I can surely ne'er forget,
The sights have stirred the mind, which I have seen,
In fancy oft, I see their beauty yet.

'Twas Edinburgh grand that woke the muse,
In darkest hours there shone a radiance bright,
When Nature bows the head in sweet repose,
My thoughts begin to rove, in silent night.

I see the castle, now in peace arrayed,
Where once the roar of guns about her pealed,
That memory in the world shall never fade,
Behold the Shrine, and sorrow is revealed.

My gaze is held in reverence profound,
A cloud of blackness rolls about my head,
Within my heart there steals a bitter wound,
That leaves me in my reverie, with the dead.

From many lips a silent prayer is said,
That seems to ease the burden as they go,
From many eyes a hallowed tear is shed,
For heroes whom the world shall never know.

They, all alike, have found their rest at last,
Their names remain upon our earthly road,
Their faces smile upon us from the past,
An honour to their Country, and their God.

A Stroke of Luck

Behold the amazing ball I played,
It almost struck the flag,
Perhaps you won't believe me dear,
I never like to brag,
My second shot I thought would sink,
I felt it in my bones,
A chap came up and asked my name,
I answered, "Bobby Jones."

Christmas

A day hath come of mirth and cheer,
A day outstanding in the year,
It's name hath lived in years before,
Thus shall it live for evermore.

I wish you joy this Christmas-tide,
And may goodluck with you abide,
Rejoice ye on this blissful morn,
On which our heavenly King was born.

After Hearing School Yarns

Now Rita, I will first impress to try and keep my cool,
I know it will be rather hard to stay by such a rule,
But, if until myself you see, your anger you delay,
Then I will bear, with sad despair, the things you have to say.

Perhaps you ought to keep it quiet and show to none at all,
Or, you should try another plan and have it in the hall,
Then when your father enters there he'll read the precious paper,
And they'll transport me to the court, for trying such a caper.

But I am giving tips away of ways to capture me,
However, we shall trust to luck, and see what we shall see,
When you attended Hurlford school at drawing you were fair,
By that I mean fit to be seen, as good as any there.

But when you started at Dunlop and drawing time had come,
A bottle was the object first, an easy thing for some,
He passed them all, right round to yours, then standing scratched his head,
"Now who's dust-bin was this one in?" I think was what he said.

However, you got on quite well until the following year,
When a lady teacher taught you who perhaps was rather queer,
But queerer still would be her class, I envy not her part,
For truly now, I don't know how, it did not break her heart.

One day the teacher left the room, but left her case therein,
Now someone had a rabbit; the trick was hardly sin,
I don't know where it came from. but where it went is clear,
Right in the case, it takes its place, among her other gear.

Then shortly after her return she starts to search about,
For something lost apparently which can't be seen throughout,
Her hand she puts inside the case but touches bunny's tail,
And with a hop it strikes the top, the teacher turning pale.

I'll mention not what happened next, I think it would be wrong,
To give it all in full detail would take me rather long,
And, other things I must omit with me they shall remain,
Unless I scrape, just for your sake, another bit again.

And now I must apologise for all that I've made known,
Next time we meet, if you forgive, I hope you are alone.
We'll quietly spend another hour on thing's we've heard and seen,
When no-one's near, to overhear, the words that pass between.

J.B.W.

I want a cure for something here,
I call the trouble rather queer,
These letters haunt me night and day,
They simply can't be thrown away,
They keep my brain a perfect whirl,
Initial letters of a girl,
Now do not say you understand,
A downright answer I demand.

She gave me notes on which to muse,
It wasn't manners to refuse,
So now I think I'll make a bend,
And work my way toward the end,
She learned to cycle, graceful style,
But rather shaky for a while,
It happened in the thoroughfare,
In Main Street, Prestwick, north of Ayr.

Two bottles, those she carried level,
As home she paddled like the devil,
Now what, you ask, did these contain,
My secretary will explain,
I thought 'twas polish of a sort,
But he can swear that it was port,
So port it's therefore got to be,
It suits much better, you'll agree.

She fell her length upon the ground,
Yet never made a single sound,
The only noise was bottles breaking,
Some people stood, the smell was taking,
A hero having viewed the sight,
Aprroaches her, and puts her right,
I don't know what the blighter said,
Perhaps he only stroked her head.

He helped her on her bike once more,
She said she wasn't really sore,
That graceful style was sent to yonder,
At such a thing you cannot wonder,
She bought tomatoes for the tea,
And homeward cycled steadily,
When eighteen inches from the gate,
She grips the brake, alas! too late.

These ripe tomatoes strike the post,
That means the household tea is lost,
Her nice white frock, see, have a deck,
It seems to be a perfect wreck,
There isn't much in any frock,
But that one now would cause a shock;
Some port, I think, she must have had,
Things shouldn't just have been so bad.

Now darling I will draw the line,
My sole is itching just like thine,
My notes are ended, John has gone,
I might have went forever on,
But thank the pope that this is over,
I hope you realise I'm sober,
The whole concern was done for you,
So with my love I'll say adieu.

Psalms - No.1

Believe ye in the Lord thy God,
O bliss his name alway,
For He His life laid down for us,
That we might live for aye.

He hath done many gracious deeds,
Yea unto all mankind,
Hath cleansed the lepers, healed the sick,
And gave sight to the blind.

Wherefore believe ye in the Lord,
For all His wondrous love,
For He that promised better days,
Even in the heaven above.

No.2

Lord thou knowest every day,
All I do, and all I say,
All my works to thee are known,
Through the ages all along.

Thou shalt be my guard and guide,
Thou art ever by my side,
Thou shalt feed me day by day,
Thou shalt take my sins away.

This, our world is full of sin,
Fears without, and pains within,
But, there be a blissful shore,
Where such pains are felt no more.

A Wedding

One night I went off to a wedding,
I went there in a nice little car,
I landed all right, about seven at night,
'Twas the best way of going, by far.

Crosshill was the sweet little village,
The wedding was held in the hall,
So right in I went, and upstairs I was sent,
As there was the wedding and ball.

The wedding performance was started,
And all went as well as could be,
The bride's cake was cut, and we all had a bit,
And then we went down for our tea.

As soon as the eating was over,
The dancing was then to begin,
So up to the hall, they made for the ball,
And very soon all was a din.

The dancing was something terrific,
I stood and I looked in the door,
Then I stepped in the hall, and I nearly did fall,
For I thought I was down through the floor.

I stood, and I looked, and I looked, and I stood,
Till the clock on the wall gave me warning,
That, if I did not go, I would jolly soon know,
I'd be late for my work in the morning.

Scotland

You've heard people boasting of countries so rare,
Of Ireland with shamrocks and England so fair,
But give me old Scotland,
And sweet songs I'll raise,
For it will I honour,
And it will I praise.

You may think about Ireland with the grass ever green,
You may talk about England with the rose in full bloom,
But three cheers for the land,
With the mountain and river,
I'll honour it now,
And I'll honour it ever.

Umbrellas

I've written poems, quite a lot,
I've studied themes in earnest thought,
But here is one I clean forgot,
Umbrellas.

A house I enter rather late,
But ere I knock I quietly wait,
The tongues are frantic in debate,
Umbrellas.

"I'm jolly sure it wasn't me,"
That's Mirn, oh well it couldn't be,
But what's the matter, come let's see,
Umbrellas.

There's surely something has gone wrong,
To whom, (we'll ask) did it belong,
The answer comes, amid the throng,
Umbrellas.

Their brother Hugh, the truth I tell,
He askes the crowd to go to hell,
For breakfast, dinner, tea as well,
Umbrellas.

His situation I have known,
I sympathise with him alone,
The others ought to mind their own,
Umbrellas.

He mends a chair to save a spill,
He makes a drawer against his will,
But constant it continues still,
Umbrellas.

From early morn till close of day,
The strife goes on, without delay,
At half a mile you'll hear them say,
Umbrellas.

'Twas Mary's, now we're in the run,
And someone's lost it, here's the fun,
The Lord have mercy on that one,
Umbrellas.

They dream about it in their bed,
A doctor ought to look their head,
That gamp, has joined the blessed dead,
Umbrellas.

The Cinema Fire

On Hogmanay 1929, while an entertainment for children was going on in a cinema in Paisley, the place caught·fire. The death roll, stated in all papers on New Year's morning, amounted to seventy.

Let not the bells of gladness ring tonight,
For winds of death and darkness hover here;
When morning suns were shining all was bright,
But mourning has begun another year.

How many are the tears of sorrow shed,
No human tongue their anguish can impart,
Three score and ten, are numbered with the dead,
And all are children, dear to someone's heart.

With happy thoughts those tender minds would fill,
Until the drastic knell did wildly toll,
The scene is o'er, and yet I see it still,
With secret sorrow, in the silent soul.

Now side by side their noble dust is laid,
In melancholy rite beneath the sod,
Their names on earth the blast of time shall fade,
But never from the presence of their God.

We mourn, but comforts arm shall now uphold,
And ease the burden of the bitter past,
Until that knell in sweetness shall be tolled,
And brightness shall be seen again, at last.

Life

How glorious is the hour of morn,
How sweet the hour of eve;
A glance I cast on time between,
What wondrous webs we weave,
Some, brilliant moments, lit with joy,
There's others dark in pain,
    One day alone,
    Like life is shown,
Let's live it o'er again.

Far in the bosom of the East,
The flickering rays of dawn,
Outspread across a smiling land,
Where they before have shone,
But, to a new-born race how fair,
To every eye how keen,
    Till clouds and haze,
    Defect the rays,
And mar the magic scene.

The light we once beheld with awe,
Is shortly overcome,
The mystic mind controls the tongue,
But oft', the mind is numb;
An angry word will lead to strife,
May thoughtless words depart,
    A loving strain,
    Is never vain,
But wins a neighbour's heart.

The hours are passing fast away,
I see the future loom,
But still pursuing let us move,
Before the dusk of doom,
When skies are bleak, and hearts are cold,
And flowers no fragrance give,
          My God, I pray,
          Take life away,
I'd rather die than live.

Our gaze is slowly Westward turned,
And lo!, the setting sun
Appears with glory as of old
When life was just begun.
From out the depths a visage pale,
Demands the shallow breath,
          The lustre fades,
          And darkness shades,
The silent vale of death.

Grief

There's times we all must turn aside,
From joy and pleasure gay,
And face the dull and weary path,
That winds through sorrow's way,
Oh, for a heart to sympathise,
A hand to wipe a tear,
In melancholy joy would shine,
In sadness, there were cheer.

Thus, when in mournful grief cast down,
The tide of hope is low,
If I could ease one heart alone,
And share its deepest woe,
To gladness would my soul return,
Whene'er I saw a smile,
And ever on I'd wend my way,
Contented, for a while.

How oft my mind, dejected, strays,
To scenes that men forget,
When ghastly gloom shall dim the sun,
For death shall conquer yet;
How glorious are the days of youth,

Or childhood, bright and free,
All these compare on Life's strange road,
And, is it vanity?

Now friends rejoice in early days,
Although my words are dull;
(My thoughts remain), but I in life,
Shall not in darkness fall,
The end that's known is clear, yet void,
For one and all the same.
The dust shall to the dust return,
And God his spirit claim.

The Cairn, Auchincruive

Unveiled 14th September 1929.

Oft have I roamed among the hills,
Where Ayr in splendour flows,
I love to watch her wind and turn,
As ever on she goes,
To hear the birds on ilka tree,
In shrill or tuneful voice,
Is comfort to the listening ear,
And makes the heart rejoice.

Some warrior here in days of yore,
Has in concealment lay;
The scene has charmed a poet's thought,
Of river, bank, and brae.
A cairn has been erected here,
Close on the river side,
In grand and honoured memory,
Of men that Scotland pride.

A noted lady of the land,
Unveiled the stately stone,
Upon a mound it has been placed,
Like knight upon his throne,
And many people gathered round,
At that appointed time,
An incident which there occurred,
Has put my words in rhyme.

Some lavender the lady held,
As to her car she went,
And as she sat in perfect grace,
Her eyes became intent;
A child beside the door she saw,
She handed out a spray,
Her lips possessed a loving smile,
That never shall decay.

Some friends when you can understand,
The story will relate,
Perhaps the little flower they'll keep,
Along with day and date.
The cairn is for remembrance sake,
These words may act the same,
In far, unknown, and future days,
They may recall, a name.

A name, or names that cared for thee,
In happy days gone by,
Reflect, but for a little space,
With far discerning eye;
That sacred beam shall then arise,
Deep, in the inward sight,
A ray, that in the darkest hour,
Dispels the shades of night.

Caught

I've lots and lots of friends you know
About the town of Ayr,
And some are just the real old sort,
And some are only fair,
And some can show themselves around,
And others can't be seen,
And some are good, and some are bad,
And some are in between.

Now this is one of those smart girls,
With all the virtues bright,
She, with her much beloved young man,
Strolled off one winter night;
There's heaps of things that did take place,
But I have singled one,
And when you hear, I know you'll say,
It takes the blinking bun.

As soon as necking time was up,
They must retrace their way,
The chap, a fresh fused bulb espies,
And hits a plan, O.K.,
He picks it up, and jogs along,
As he, the scene forebodes,
Then with a bang, right at her heel,
The ——— thing he explodes.

The language, Jenny used, my friends,
I really can't repeat,
She fully shocked the neighbourhood,
And put them off their meat;
She threw her arms above her head,
And jerked her radial vein,
And for the next few days, I know,
She quietly bore the strain.

But after all, I think myself,
It went with perfect swing,
It made the damsel realise,
She was a living thing;
And thus dispelled the charming love,
That she had made, so well,
By telling her poor lover straight,
He was to go to hell.

To Comfort

Now are the shades of evening falling fast,
The last strange streaks of daylight almost gone,
The hours of labour for the day are past,
And I am left in silence, and alone.

To you I write in melancholy strain,
In sympathy and comfort, if I may,
But not to bring your sickened soul to pain,
Or paint the skies that livid leaden grey.

Here is a starlit night, a glorious morn,
Descending, still descending, and shall bloom;
E'en through the darkness shall the light be born,
And joy shall reign, where rested bitter gloom.

Far from the haunts of this incessant grief,
Hope must outspread His wide triumphant wing;
Hope that shall gain the weary heart relief,
And win the love, of Heaven's Eternal King.

A Big Event

One fine day in Glasgow,
There was a great Hallabaloo,
A rhinoceros and a hippo,
Had broken from the zoo.

The big iron gates were open,
They ran out like a shot;
I thought that they were captured,
But the rest said they were caught.

The clever man who caught them,
Was just about the Co.,
His laces both had broken,
And he had to let them go.

The rhinoceros and the hippo,
They ran away in style,
I heard the people saying,
They ran a thousand mile.

But I found out they did not,
For a little dog named Haigie,
Hunted them from place to place,
Till it landed them in Craigie.

Longing

June 1928.

When darkness spreads across the distant hills
And Nature's eyelids close in sweet repose,
At such an hour my soul with ardour fills,
My wandering mind in inspiration grows.
Behold the eyes of childhood smile on me,
That heart of love contains no deadly wound,
I long, in deep solemnity, to see,
My gaze is held in reverence profound;
No evil ever blurred that tender mind,
No blackness ever loomed above that brow,
Those years, my thoughts are tracing far behind,
I heave a sigh at recollections now;
Regardless of the future with its store,
When days of grief were days you never knew;
Where melancholy lurks the heart is sore,
But where a light appears let man pursue,
A tear of sorrow oft at times is shed,
But never let them flow a ceaseless wave,
For joy and sorrow both alike are led,
And laid within a cold and silent grave.
Then walk in joy and gloom shall disappear,
A loving smile is light upon the road,
Where childhood smiles in innocence sincere,
That smile is more than pleasing unto God;
Thus, while I muse in silence and retreat,
Within my inner heart there steals a pain,
My thoughts are moved in reminiscence sweet,
This night, I long to be a child again.

Snowdrops

I never saw the acting done,
But this I'm told is true:-
A nice wee lassie dressed in white,
Except for something blue,
Once gave a recitation, thus,
The story I renew.

She did it at a soiree,
'Twas many years ago,
She had to stand upon a chair,
To make a little show,
She had a basket full of flowers,
Of snow drops, don't you know.

And then she laid it off her chest,
And made the rafters ring,
About the pretty flowers that bloom,
In days of early spring,
Some people in the audience,
Their cookies meant to fling.

And what a swank she thought she was,
Although I didn't see,
She couldn't look at common folk,
The like of you or me,
If she had toppled off the chair,
There would have been a spree.

So now the Snowdrops bow their heads,
And gaze on earth in gloom,
And pale as death they waft and wave,
As if they saw their doom,
That night the shock was rather much,
They almost ceased to bloom.

Hope and Friendship

If all the wishes I could wish
Would come a trifle true,
I'd wish them o'er a thousandfold,
For no-one else but you.

But what's the use of vain deceit,
It ever ends in woe,
Contented be with where you stand,
And aim for where you'd go.

Thus would I live with patient hope,
Though darkness lies before,
For once a loving heart is lost,
There's nothing can restore.

True friendship, faith, and hope, in life,
Make loves reflection shine;
Or simply, just when one true heart,
Has confidence in thine.

A Birthday Greeting

When dull November's blast is heard,
With weird and eerie moan,
In darkest hours my mind returns,
Enraptured and alone,
To where a heart in silence beats,
My thoughts forever stray,
Tonight in placid pensive mood,
A greeting they convey.

May happiness and luck be yours,
In years that are to come,
When sadness falls may that be slight,
And star dispel the gloom,
May comfort's arms be led to yours,
When you in grief shall mourn,
To ease the burden pressing sore,
Till joy and hope return.

'Tis just a birthday wish expressed,
I hope it may be real;
The bitter pains that rend the heart,
A wish can never heal,
But where a kindly word is heard,
In sympathetic strain,
It stimulates the weary step,
And makes you smile again.

Pudding for Breakfast

'Twas in the morning early,
Before the sun had shone,
A girl of my acquaintance,
Was duly knocked upon.

Her mother thought to please her,
Or shut her face instead,
She'd just make up her breakfast,
And hand it into bed.

I never asked the contents,
I merely have been told,
A lump of currant pudding,
Was on a plate behold.

She had a spoon to eat it,
I tell the truth indeed;
She scattered it about the bed,
Like someone sowing seed.

And then she made the limp excuse,
She wasn't right awake,
Well every morning after this,
I'd see she gets a shake.

But watch you don't offend her,
While sitting near the grate,
She'll lift the poker right away,
And let you have its weight.

The Curly "Tale" of a Pig

Ye farmers, everyone take heed,
This yarn I tell is truth indeed,
Of how a pig was lost one night,
And how 'twas traced, and brought to light;
Of how I wandered far and near,
Was sometimes there, and sometimes here,
And never a one that I could see,
Could help my soul in agony.

On Tuesday nights 'tis well nigh great.
When market days are wearin' late,
'Twas such a night as this in question,
Gave Andrew Chalmers indigestion;
A man, (a mere stone-throw from Ayr),
Had brought this pig, at that said fair.

Yet someone took that pig astray,
And floated it up Neilston way;
The cry got up, the folks were smart,
A large search-party scoured the mart.
One pig was left, asleep and weary,
The wrong pig's off, now here's a query.

The books were turned and showed quite clear,
That Hughie Wilson's name was there,
He'd got a farm up that direction,
A short time since, I'd better mention,
And now, he deems it is his duty,
To buy this bulky sleeping beauty,
Whilst lying cuddled 'mong the hay,
The wrong pig's taken, right away.

This man that bought the pig that hopped it,
From his dear wife I think he'd copped it;
Back to the auctioneers he rattles,
And for his pig severely battles.
Then my instructions clear, are made,
But ah; my route is vaguely laid.

The farm, they cannot name to me,
And I am left to find it, - see.
"They think nae on the lang Scots miles,
The mosses, waters, slaps, and stiles"
That lie between me and my goal,
But on and on I seem to roll.

At Lugton, first, I tell my tale,
Enquiries seem of no avail,
I ask, and ask, of many more,
Till I have asked at least a score.
Well, here we are at Uplawmoor,
A place I'd never seen before,
I halt at a policeman's dwelling,
And soon to him my tale I'm telling,
He phones to one, he phones another,

But no man knows this unknown brother,
At last; here's one that's bound to know,
He rings the blacksmith up, "Hullo!"
"Yes, five miles onward there you'll get,
The pig, on which your heart is set.

"But that's not all your worry over,"
Says this P.C., "You'd better hover,
This road is one that's not too level,
And twisted as the very Devil.
Sit down a blink," to me he beckoned,
"I'll just be with you in a second."
"By jove," says I, "That's jolly good."
And off we set in better mood.

We reached the farm, they're all in bed,
We raised a noise would wake the dead,
Then, out comes Hughie smelling trouble,
And swore that he was seeing double;
Of course, when we explained our mission,
He saw at once the real position;
Past cattle, hens and ducks and geese,
Behold our pig, "The Golden Fleece."

Back with our prize to Uplawmoor,
We won't forget that night, I'm sure,
We had our tea, a crack, a story,
Then off for home, in all our glory.
As Auchincruive was drawing nigh,
A strange faint light I did espy,
It proved to be the rightful owner,
Relieved once more to look upon her,
His "Better-half" my praises sung,
As round my neck her arms she flung,
Thence to the pig they both went flying,
And by its side they soon were lying.

'Twas when I saw them there repose,
It made me think of beds and clothes,
Thus, softly stealing from the show,
My work was done, I then could go,
Since then my thoughts have travelled wide,
But some strange sound condemned my pride,
In Fancy's ear, when I recline,
I hear the guzzling of the swine.

The Picnic

It was a Sunday afternoon,
The sun was shining grand,
I started up the good old car,
I don't mean second-hand,
I rattled on New Cumnock way,
I've often been the road,
And, at Glen Afton right away,
I got a hefty load.

Four girls I lifted, that was all,
The car was almost full,
We sailed along among the hills,
And saw the black sheep's wool,
I stopped at places one or two,
For ices, chips and stamps,
But Edith made me stop in style,
You're wrong, it was with cramp.

She was as sick's a collie pup,
That's newly left its mother;
Says I, "Now just step right outside,
Should there be any other."
Still, all the same, that put her right,
We soon again were going,
But on that same said spot, I fear,
The grass will cease from growing.

A little further up the road,
She got a drink of water,
And there and then she took her "temp."
In case she might get hotter,
So here and now I'll draw the line,
I hope you're all delighted,
But, in the future, take my tip,
And do not get excited.

To M.C.R.

30th May 1936.

When you awoke, the Morning Star,
In beauty gave you light,
That little Star you said was Hope,
And you were nearly right.

But in that Star there must be Faith,
And trust, when it is gone,
For though the clouds of darkness come,
There also comes a dawn.

That Star requires our Faith my child,
Then Hope is His design,
Still brighter shines His strongest ray,
Of perfect Love divine.

Mairburn Waddin

Christmas Day, 1940.

We've seen him in the Market Square,
Whiles buyin' calves or stirkies there,
At every special cattle fair,
        We've seen him biddin',
But noo we've got him in a snare,
        And I'm no' kiddin'.

At times he's in the Auction Ring,
Sellin' twa queys, or sic like thing,
Up goes the haun, "Anither wing,
        I've got tae get,
Before I'll sell at that, by jing!
        I'll eat ma hat."

At every farmers' sale that's near,
He's share tae be. Whiles things are dear,
"We'll gang an' hae a gless of beer,"
        He'll say tae Jake,
Then roon the corner wi a sweer,
        For auld times sake.

At plewin' matches whaur is he?
I hear him, though I canna see.
"Haud on, John, damn ye, in a wee,
        Ye're gettin' crookit."
The laugh's on us, John, at this spree,
        Since he's been hookit.

But Tam, the best o' luck tae you,
And Grace, my wishes ever true,
Lang spared, as doon the field ye plew,
        The rig o' life,
May troubles in their turn be few,
        As man and wife.

There's Nothing Wrong With Nature

Written to Bill Paterson, Christmas 1941, using his words, "There's nothing wrong with Nature," said at the caravan, Carsphairn.

There's nothing wrong with Nature, friend,
Or, with the earth, from end to end,
As onward through this life we wend,
        We hear the song,
From the high hills it may descend,
        "There's nothing wrong."

I walked the mountain road today,
Past tall, dark, pines that clothed the way,
The sky o'erhead was cold and grey,
        But all along,
I heard those whispering branches say,
        "There's nothing wrong."

Far off, beside yon distant hill,
There rises many a water rill,
That foams and rushes past the mill,
        Where I belong,
Yet, while it chatters, murmers still,
        "There's nothing wrong."

'Tis man that's marred this earthly plain,
And seethed her sons in bitter pain,
All that he seeks is worldly gain,
        There to be strong,
Nature can answer this refrain,
        "There's something wrong."

To Mr & Mrs J. MacKay

on their Silver Wedding, 27th April 1942.

Five and twenty years, ah! yes,
Short has been the way,
Happiness has followed on,
Since that happy day,
Since that day they one were made,
Time is marching on,
Strange, it is the way of life,
Five and twenty gone.

Just a milestone, that is all,
Night is far in shade,
All the best is yet to be,
That's how life was made.
Rise, and let us onward press,
Till the goal be won,
There is many tasks to do,
Though five and twenty gone.

O'er this road they have been blessed,
They can ne'er forget;
Hills they know are still to climb,
Naught has failed them yet.
Carry on when days are dull,
Courage, and be strong,
Life has sweetness yet to give,
Though five and twenty gone.

May the joy that has been theirs,
Bide for years to come,
Shining, as the mid-day sun,
Breaks the clouds of gloom,
This my wish for them tonight,
From my heart I pour,
Health and happiness throughout,
Five and twenty more.

Song

Tune- "The Nameless Lassie" (music by Alex MacKenzie).

Fu' mony are the joys we had,
When life was fresh and young,
The sound of music filled the air,
The songs were sweet we sung,
When love's young dream bestirs the heart,
O'erflowing in a song,
In these blythe days o' yesteryear,
The blood was running strong.

When coortin' by the wee moss burn,
Our love was warm and true,
I recollect these hours o' bliss,
When life and love were new.
The burn still babbles doon the glen,
The channels deeper wear,
The mark o' time is on oor broo,
Since, sweethearts, we were there.

Fond memories ever fill my thoughts,
Great treasures rich and kind,
The gifts that gold can never buy,
Are banked within my mind,
And still this constant love remains,
This tribute of the past,
In growing old this is my song,
As long as life shall last.

The Sewing Machine

This tale begins along while back,
At Brocklehill, when ca'ing the crack,
Ae Sunday nicht, when by the fire,
Talkin' o' things aroon the shire,
Ye ken hoo wives go bletherin' on,
Aye, sometimes even on the 'phone,
That nicht the crack was goin' wi' cheer,
When this wee bit I chanced tae hear,
Says Mrs. Gibb, "Noo listen frien',
Ma name's in for a shewing machine,
An all-electric one, just swell,
That shews the things like flames o' hell."

"My," say the wife, "Is that no' great,
My word you're getting up to date.
But tell me this, and tell me true,
What are ye shewin' wi' the noo?"
Says Mrs. Gibb, "It is a Singer,
But, fegs, it still can go its dinger,
It's shewed mair stuff that tongue can tell,
But gettin' auld, jist like masel'."
"Well," says the wife, "I'll make a dale,
This aul' machine'll be for sale,
Whene'er you get your new ane set,
The first chance o' the aul' I'll get."
Long months ha'e passed - I'll say thirteen,
Since last I heard o' this machine,
Till jist the ither efternin,
When doon frae Brocklehill I spin,
Richt in a sheugh, beside a tree,
I spy something - syne stop tae see.
An auld and roosted shewing machine,
The worst I'm sure ye've ever seen,
Long, long ago, had been flung oot,
And there had lain for years, nae doobt,
Perchance this gadget now rescued,
Your granny's granny's claes hae shewed,
Or, in some mansion had its place,
When underclothes were trimmed wi' lace,
Or, dwalt in some wee humble cot,
When claes were claes, no' easy got,
A tear micht trickle frae her e'e,
Should some auld body gaze on ye,
That plied wi' thread and gart ye shew,
When she was young, and you were new,
But, come awa' alang wi' me,
We're goin' tae hae a dampt guid spree,
Try an' forget your past, for faith,
You're worth five pound, as sure as daith.
At Raggethill the yarn I spin,
Tae cadge some stuff tae row it in,
Thence on my way I do proceed,
Lastly to ca' in at Stran'heid,
Again this yarn I did outpour,
To Jimmy, jist outside the door,
His wife came oot and heard it tae,
Says I tae her, "This job you'll dae,
Some extra paper get, and string,
And see if you can row this thing

Intae a parcel neat enough,
And I'll get hame and dae my stuff."
I landed hame and taen ma tea,
Then, sat and read, for jist a wee,
Then in I voice I says, quite green,
"I've got a blinkin' shewing machine.
Fae Mrs. Gibb. She says to me,
'This aul' machine I've got for ye,
The wife, of coorse, she will hae min',
I promised her it lang, lang syne,'"
"Oh, heavens, aye," the wife says, "Jing,
I clean forgot aboot the thing,
Go oot the noo and fetch it roon,
I'm pleased she mind tae send it doon."
Thence tae the shed of coorse I gang,
(It disnae tak me very lang),
I plunked the parcel on her knee,
She luks it ower, and then says she,
"It hasnae got a box, I see,
But, the jiner, he'll mak ane for me.
Did Mrs Gibb, I ocht tae say,
Mention the price o' this the day?"
"Deed, aye," says I, "She tellt me it,
But hummed and hawed for quite a bit.
Five pounds she says, wis whit I thocht,
It cost far mair when it was bocht,
Five pounds," says I, "Is quite okay,
I hinnae on me whit would dae."
"Hoots man," says she, "That's richt enough,
I'm owin' her for a lot o' stuff,"
Noo, by this time the knot did ease,
As this bit scrap sat on her knees,
"Haud oan," says I, "Frae whit I'm tellt,
Five pounds is jist below the belt."
"Here, hark tae whit I've got tae say,"
She says tae me, "Noo richt away,
Tae some saleroom I micht gae through,
And buy a braw machine like new,
And pey five pounds, or eight, or nine,
And think that I had done quite fine,
Then when I get it hame at first,
Discover that its guts is bust,
But this machine that here does lie,
I know that it's the real Mackay."
"'Nuff said," says I, "Well spoken too,"
Wi' that, the article's in view,

The paper drappit on the flair,
The shewing machine was lyin' there.
She looked at it, but never spoke,
She saw of coorse it was a joke,
Then in a voice as clear's a bell,
She send's machine and me tae hell,

Limericks

There was a young fellow from Ayr,
Who was walking along unaware,
He was wheelin' a pram,
And he snaffled a ham,
But they caught him in Burns Statue Square.

There's a ferm up the road, Garryhorn,
Whaur a wee fella Davie was born,
Wi' an air gun and slugs,
He was shootin' wee speugs,
Ae day I was up wi' some corn.

Ye a' ken the lad fae Carnavel,
He aince tied a dug tae the table,
The dug kinna' loupit,
And the dishes a' coupit,
And noo it gets shut in the stable.

Barn Dance

"Kirkcudbrightshire is next to Ayrshire, but they do things different down there. We were invited down to Blawquhairn, at Dalry, to a barn dance, in aid of Carsphairn Kirk."

Ye hing yer coat up in the byre,
The done thing in Kirkcudbrightshire,
Ower ony trevis hing your coat,
But try an' min' whit kin' ye've got,
For, if ye dinna tak ma tip,
You'll get it lyin' in the grip,
A lad I ken nearhaun' Carsphairn,
He hisna awfu' much tae learn,
At haunlin' sheep he's to the fore,
At dug-hunts, he can always score,
But there the nicht I chanced tae see,
He had a beauty on his knee,

She was a smasher a' thegither,
And no' a great time left her mither,
He wrocht her weel, never did abuse her,
And squeezed her in ahin the bruiser.
It's worth your money, I'm no' kiddin,
Tae tak your lass roon by the midden,
The smell's no' maybe up your street,
But if ye mind tae dicht yer feet,
The cool nicht air will soon dispel,
The rotten kinda stinkin' smell,
Some auld anes that are no sae fit,
Oot winchin in the silage pit,
Anither lad ahin' the rucks,
Has snaffled ane o' Arnold's jucks,
He caught it by the feet sae yellow,
And he shouted tae anither fellow,
"Here, pu' its neck, and let's get crackin',
We've got tae keep this juck frae quackin'"

Wull MacLellan's Pony

"Noo if ye see a pownie, boy,
That's goin' kinna chape," says he,
"As long's ye think the price is richt,
Ye can fetch ane doon tae me."
"Oh, man," says I, "I saw ane Wull,
The colour o't was grey,"
"Oh damt," says he. "The very dab,
I'll pay ye right away."
"Oh jist a meenit, Wull," says I,
"His tale was long and thin,"
"Hoots, whit's aboot its tale?" says he,
"Was it goin' quite soon ahin?"
"Oh, aye," says I. "As soon's a bell,
But it lugs were long and flat,
In fact, it was a cuddy, Wull,
Would it maitter much for that?"

Newton Stewart Tup Sales

Dear freens, and neebours met aroon,
Here in Dalry, or St John's toon,
I gether that ye've a' been doon
At some tup sale,
And noo ye're bletherin', boastin', roon'
Yer gless o' ale.

I understand frae whit ye say,
Some high class sheep were there that day,
You lads could value them and say,
Just in a trice,
"There's ane ower there should dae,
Auld freen, at sicna price."

Wull Wallace there, he's gaun tae bid,
O' cash this day he must get rid,
A braw sheep's chapped, at thirty quid,
Tae Fingland's name,
He'll dae the ewes a power o' guid,
When he gets hame.

I like the rams among my flock,
That dae their job like one o' clock,
And no' thae sheepy, shaggy brock,
That prowl aroon',
That only hiv a wee bit snock,
And then sit doon.

Noo, in the Spring, when Winter's gane,
Wi' a' her snaw, and wind and rain,
When lambs are skippin' ower the plain,
It's then we'll trace,
If this same ram was worth its keep,
At Fingland's place.

But should the rotter prove your foe,
Wi' only silly lambs tae show,
Just hit him yin, a hefty blow,
Wi' ocht ye've got,
And, when he's doon and lyin' low,
Just cut his throat.

The fleece will dae some hawker chiel,
The horns for crooks, the braes tae speil,
The mutton on him should day weel,
        Tae hiv a feed,
Nae mair he'll traik aboot the fiel',
        Tae butt or breed.

Wha's spared my lads among us here,
Tae see things through anither year,
Micht meet, I hope, in social sphere,
        This nicht again,
Whaur freenship's haun is held sincere,
        It must remain.

The above poem was written by Allan Ramsay at the request of Robbie Murray (descendant of Professor Alexander Murray of Dunkitterick). It was to be read out at a meeting of shepherds and farmers at a hotel in Dalry, where a competition was to be held for a poem based on Newton Stewart tup sale. Allan won the prize of a shepherd's crook. Unfortunately Robbie Murray could not attend, due to the death of his father, but sent Allan the following verses later:

Dear Allan Ramsay frae Annbank,
A cup o' tea I've newly drank,
Here in the armchair I ha'e sank,
        My pen I've ta'en,
And now, Sir, I maun kindly thank,
        You for your poem.

Your verses, they had done the trick,
I'm pleased you won the walking stick,
When loadening ewes you'll aye can slick,
        A ewe that turns,
At poetry makin' you can lick,
        Them a' but Burns.

I hope that Fingland's tup does weil,
And aye keeps fit the taps tae spiel,
Can rin jist like the very Deil,
        As fast's a taxi,
And never jump oot o' his fiel',
        Coup, droon, or braxy.

And when his grass it needs a tap,
Just hark tae this I'll tell you what,
Twa loads o' cattle on him drap,
Next year in June,
It'll pey as weil as ony tup,
At thirty poun'.

I missed the dug hunt at Dalry,
Next time we meet I'll tell ye why,
When passin' through if ye are dry,
Just drink your fill,
And tell the publican that I,
Will pay the bill.

And when you're hikin' on the hills,
By wimplin' streams and mountain rills,
Whaur grows the bent and heather bells,
In summer's heat,
The "Forrest", aye your belly fills,
Ca' in for meat.

Some nicht we three will break the tether,
And in the Clachan we'll forgether,
Fingland, you and I thegither,
Ye will na' weary,
It's ae fool lauchin' at anither,
That mak's us cheery.

So here's a haun' for freendship's sake,
Just grup it ticht and gae't a shake,
I hope you aye your meals can take,
An' never worry,
May oor acquaintance never break,
Yours, Robert Murray.

The Pentalina

June, in Summer 1972.

Perhaps, my freen, you've crossed the sea,
To Mull, Iona, or Tiree,
Perchance on some fine summer day,
You've sailed frae Largs tae Rothesay bay,
Or maybe in a Scottish Queen,
To foreign shores you may have been,
There's varied ships, there's sturdy crews,
Rafts, yachts, tugs, liners and canoes,
Great vessels, and wee rowin' boats,
But, have ye been tae John-o-Groats?
There, tak your wife and weans a sail,
This boat goes like a bloomin' whale.
St Margaret's Hope, its destination,
Wi' John-o-Groats the mainland station.
Whit make o' ship - you'll hiv tae speer,
Ask Alfie, - he's the engineer.
It's no much longer than it's wide,
Named "Pentalina" on its side,
Bill Banks the skipper's lots o' pluck,
He keeps her floatin' like a juck,
Bill Sinclair is the bosun too,
These are the mainsprings o' the crew,
It wasna sic a rotten day,
The ain we went tae Ronaldsay,
On oor return, tae tell the truth,
The sea was foamin' at the mooth.
While Bill the skipper scanned the decks,
Whiles he had on, whiles aff, his specs,
Although the wind was dour and chill,
"Let's have a bash at it," says Bill,
And sae we left, 'mid sleet and rain,
Tae ploo the angry ocean main,
The "Pentalina" chearilee,
Gaed chirlin' through the ragin' sea,
Yes sir, that boat did really well,
Divin' through waves as big's hersel',
It was the glorious month o' June,
When young yins go their honeymoon,
When golden suns should ever shine,
When he micht whisper, "You are mine."
Not so on this particular trip,
He's apt tae gie his wife the pip,

'Twas just aroon the longest day,
Wi' nae sunshine, I'm sad to say,
The year o' Nineteen Seventy-Two,
The summer jist a richt blue-doo,
I sat as quate's a new born lamb,
And tellt masel' the sea was calm,
The ship at times would rock and roll,
But Bill, he kept her in control,
At last, amid the howlin' gale,
I saw the coast through mist and hail,
When e'er my feet are firm and sure,
You'll never see ma heels for stoor,
Through "Pentalina's" tough windscreen,
At John-o-Groats, stood Johnnie Green,
Nae better cronie ever came,
Tae lead the trauchled wanderer hame.

This is my own, my Native Land

(Johnnie Walker Scots Poetry Competition)

I cling to the land of my birthright,
The land o' the Scottish bluebell,
        The pairt I lo'e best,
        Where I lay in the nest,
Concealed in a quiet lonely dell.
For there I was born in December,
Wi' the sang o' the Doon wimplin' clear:
        By her banks and her braes,
        There I spent happy days,
Long ago, in Life's Spring o' the year.

That hame was the pride o' my childhood,
A wee cosy neat, but and ben,
        Just an' odd mile or twa,
        Whaur, 'mid January's snaw,
Was born the maist famous o' men.
He wrote praise o' his dear native country,
O' the herts that he lo'ed, leal and true,
        Robert Burns was his name,
        In the great Scroll of Fame,
He lives, never old, ever new.

Not only by Ayrshire I linger,
Although in my blood it runs strong,
        From the east to the west,
        If put to the test,
For ilk pairt there's a guid Scottish song.
I have travelled oft times in the Highlands,
'Mong the islands I wander away,
        By the crofter's peat fire,
        Is a dear heart's desire,
At the close o' the lang summer's day.

The Book of Life

I scanned the book of life today,
And turned a special page,
I read the name there - Maurice Brown,
My friend of "Hermitage",
I brought him lambs, I brought him ewes,
And other varied stock,
But most of all my joy was full,
To simply sit and talk,
To his dear partner of this earth,
A lass I never knew,
My deepest sympathy sincere,
I now convey to you.
And in the days of "yet to be",
A Higher hand above,
Will guide you always safely through,
With everlasting love.

National Farmers Union of Scotland

Annual Dinner, March 1996.

The N.F.U. of Scotland,
Have gathered in Belleisle,
Frae a' the airts the win' can blaw,
Aroon oor Scottish isle.

You're always welcome here in Ayr,
Famous for Ayrshire kye,
Bullocks and heifers, various breeds,
Rare guid Scotch Beef forby.

Renowned by oor dear local bard,
Immortal Rabbie's name,
Weil kent through oot the hale wide world,
"Burns", - o' poetic fame.

Weil fed you'll be this nicht nae doot,
On guid Scotch hamely fare,
Wi milk and meal and black face lamb,
In this auld toon o' Ayr.

Twa hunner years since Rabbie died,
A genius, that's for sure,
He gave this earth a treasure store,
Perfected, rich and pure.

Met here a' Scottish fermin' chiels,
Here by the banks o' Doon,
This is a milestone on life's way,
A jewel in the croon.

A hearty welcome, yin an' a,
Sincerely, warm and true,
Frae - Scotland's National Farmers team,
Kent as the N.F.U.

Home Thoughts From Abroad

A Scottish laddie gets mairret overseas.
(Written for his young friends now resident in Chicago, U.S.A.)

Dear Ian lad, frae Ayr auld toon,
I hear your waddin's comin' roon,
Your Pa and Ma - doon whaur they bide,
The Border clachan o' Chirnside,
Telt me the news has spread and cairret,
That you, dear lad, plan tae get mairret.

In Boston Auld Kirk, ower the sea,
That's whaur the waddin' has tae be,
The parson there withoot a doot,
Frae oor Kilmarnock claims a root,
The same as Burns that poet chiel,
Wha fermed at Lochlea and Mossgiel,
And got his weil-earned sma' commission,
Frae his Kilmarnock first edition.

Sae back tae Scotia cast yer e'e,
Tae Ayr auld toon when you were wee;
Although, dear lad, you're far awa,
You've won a lassie sweet and braw,
"The Sanctuary" hame, that's whaur ye bide,
And Janet, ever by your side,
'Twill be the happiest shiel ye'll ken,
As snug's a Scottish but and ben.

Janet, - a nurse o' high degree,
Plans a' the best is yet to be,
Indeed, that's oor desire for you,
Wishes frae Scotland warm and true,
Blessings to both sincerely sent,
For health, and love, and sweet content.

To Margaret and Bob

All Nature is most wonderful,
The grass, the trees, the flowers,
Take time away from storm and strife,
In restful peaceful hours,
The sweetness of the garden air,
When evening shadows close,
The peace that fills the scented breeze,
Of a red on yellow rose,
To you dear Margaret and Bob,
Our fondest love is sent,
And, may the Garden of your dreams,
Bring joy and sweet content.

Downieston's Joke

There's Downieston, I see him whiles, that's when he calls on Ben,
Whene'er he has a special job, he nabs him noo and then.
He went richt roon the hoose ae day, tae ca' at his back door,
And there was Mrs Welsh hersel', she was washin' oot the floor.

Tom saw her hin' en' stickin' oot as sweet's a bantie egg,
And fegs it was a gie near thing he meant tae catch her leg,
But wi' a juick she dodged him richt, he never touched her limb,
When she cam' ben and said tae Ben, it was a' the same tae him.

To Mr & Mrs Galloway

On the occasion of their Golden Wedding, 12th March 1971.

No hand can stay the march of time,
Or give us back the by-gone days,
'Tis best that way, and so,
In memory we recall some scenes,
Of fifty years ago.

A youth, a maid, a trysting place,
Perhaps a stile, perhaps a kiss,
Then Cupid draws his bow,
An arrow speeds straight to the mark,
Full fifty years ago.

Comes then a day two hands are clasped,
Two hearts are joined to beat as one,
Through days of weal or woe,
They plighted troth, "Till death do part",
Yes, fifty years ago.

The years slip past and family ties,
Bring happiness and likewise cares,
Today their pride will show,
How best that union was for them,
Made fifty years ago.

If hills were steep each pulled their weight,
And trusted God the top to reach,
With faces all aglow,
No setback could young spirits quench,
Nigh fifty years ago.

To Mrs Pringle

After the death of her husband, the Revd. A. Pringle of Stair.

I went alone myself today,
Around the haunts at Stair,
The birds were lost within the groves,
Deep silence filled the air.
My heart was sad, I did not sing,
As I am wont to do,
I had a feeling sore within,
With golden thoughts of you.
But, my dear lass I surely know,
A Higher Hand above,
Will guide you always safely through,
With everlasting love.

Trip to Orkney

Dear freens, if you hae time tae spare,
Sit roon the fire, draw in your chair,
And I will spin a yarn I ken,
Will gart your hair staun up on en'.

Three cronies and yours truly tae,
Decide we'll hae a holiday,
Each member votes, and all agree,
Tae Orkney island we will flee.

Their names I'll gie and mak' things clearer,
First Marr, he is a bullock rearer,
Fu' mony prizes he has won,
Wi' bullocks weighing near a ton.

A decent kin' o' country chiel,
I like the cratur unco weil,
He volunteers, a' on his ain,
Tae get the tickets for the plane,
Poor chap, he does things in a hurry,
And finds himsel' wi' weeks o' worry.

Of course I paid, and smartly did,
And quietly slipped him hauf a quid,
He said that some were sweert tae pey,
But och, his memory's gi'in' wey.

Then second, Alex frae Pinmore,
A hell o' a boy tae sleep and snore.
In oor schule days although lang syne,
Fu' mony are the tares I min'.

And then Jim Young, a cheery loon,
He has a ferm no' faur frae Troon,
A richt guid freen and hard tae bate,
As long's you keep him on the straight.

The day arrives, we leave our home,
We make for Renfrew aerodrome,
As there we sit and talk and yap,
They want a real trust-worthy chap.

A fellow wise, but never rash,
Tae keep the books and pay the cash.
I got the job, and all admit,
I made a damned good job of it!

At two p.m. this little band,
Was landed in a foreign land,
The air was chill, the wind by fegs,
Gaed chirlin' up your trooser legs.

The bus for Kirkwall, just the job,
Relieved me o' the first six bob.
We reached hotel a' feelin' weil,
And polish off a first class meal.

We then slip oot and hire a car,
And for a driver, pick the Marr,
This motor loupit tae its wark,
It couldna hauf get aff its mark.

Marr belted on that nocht could pass,
And ocht that met us on the grass,
I'm certain sure, had we been there,
Say for a week - no' ony mair,
A' ither drivers, sure as God,
Wad hae put their motors aff the road!

Next mornin' we are on our way,
Tae try oor luck on Loch Harray,
Ten miles we go in oor auld tub,
Wi' fishin' rods and bags o' grub.

We reach oor destination shin,
We hire twa boats, insteed o' yin,
We fix the outboard then and there,
And steer the barque for - Hell knows where!

The ither boat was left ahin,
For ootboards we hae only yin,
Alex and I were left tae row,
Whiles makin' grun', but awfu' slow.
Hooever we were quite content,
We caught some fish and on we went.

The ither boat was gaun full blatter,
Trailin' the minnows through the watter.
Ah freens, it grieves me a' thegither,
Tae see fish murdered hell for leather.

My heart at once wi' pity fills,
Tae see heucks fankled roon their gills,
It gars me greet tae see such vice,
But they want troots at ony price.

The following day was kin' o' breezy,
And rowin', it was ocht but easy.
Marr and masel' were pumpit dune,
We were in fact for packin' in.

We'd rowed oor ship for oors on en',
Like twa hauf-glaikit fishermen,
When to our starboard side we spy,
Baith Young and Eccles beltin' by.

Ahoy! we cry, two total wrecks,
And sure enough they save oor necks.
We fling a rope, all things secure,
They trail us up the loch like stoor.

The outboard's roaring tae some tune,
And we are divin' up and doon,
Jim says my een are wide wi' fricht,
Says he, "Calm doon, you're quite a'richt."

Says I, "By heavens, I've the shakers,
When oor boat strikes they monstrous breakers,
Wi' spray, this boat is like a trough,
We micht as weil be in the loch."

They drop the rope and let us go,
Sayin' "All the best" and "Cheerio",
Says I tae Marr, "Here tak' an oar,
And you and I will hit the shore.

We've never ever been yet beat,
It's time we had a bite o' meat."
We're makin' grun' wi' every draw,
The bankin's no' that faur awa'.

Landed at last, oh whit a strain,
My body's achin' every bane.
A cup o' tea, a scone and cheese,
Will steady up your shakin' knees.
A' efternin, withoot a doot,
We caught a lot o' bonnie troot.

'Twas ten o' clock, or maybe mair
Before we left the loch, I'm shair.
Marr drivin' fast the old bone shaker,
At narrow bridge, near met his Maker.

My een I shut and says, "Here goes!"
And hoo he jookit heaven knows.
In ony case we're hale and hearty,
Into hotel - a happy party.

Our meal is ready - soup for four,
We supped, and could have supped some more,
The second course - whit is this noo?
No' even Eccles has a clue!

I'm sittin' lukin' quite sedate,
Says I, "It's lobsters on yer plate."
Then Marr and Young thegither spoke,
"If we eat that we'll hae the boke."

Alex and I were game tae try,
"For Pete's sake, have a bash," says I,
And though we've dined on better fare,
We chewed it till oor jaws were sair.

That nicht, when a' were cuddled doon,
I lay awake and watched the moon.
I gazed at that entrancing sight,
Till the sma' 'oors o' Summer's night.

I then decided - break the rules,
And waken those three sleeping fools,
This cannot pass, I must unfold,
This scene worth more than much fine gold.

I reckon they will all be glad,
And call me such a mindful lad,
Instead of that, by heavens not,
They damned near kilt me on the spot!

They ca'd me names I can't repeat,
They kicked me wi' their big bare feet,
But when the picture met their eyes,
They quickly did apologise.

"Sorry we are for what we said,
And glad that we got out of bed."
Thus night and day I take their snash,
Attend their wants and pay the cash.

The time slipped by wi' tentless heid,
But happy days we had indeed,
We got oor troots cleaned, smoked, divided,
The treasurer, as usual, peyed it!

The hire o' caur was pretty dear,
I read the bill, the price was clear.
Into the heid yin I got stuck,
And asked him whit was gaun for luck.
Wi' grunts and groans he did agree,
Tae tak' us tae the plane buckshee.

When at the aerodrome we sat,
I noticed Eccles face was wat,
I thocht at first he meant tae greet,
But soon discovered it was sweet.

I passed the cash book gently roon,
And each yin gaed a mumpin' soun',
Says I, "It's plain enough tae see,
The answer's richt, divide by three."

Young, fair enough I must admit,
Hauls wallet oot and opens it,
He counts the flaffers, sure but slow,
An odd new fiver lurks below.

Marr shouts, "Hell, stop!" and gies a glower,
"We're swindled, it's divide by fower."

"Tae damn," says I, "I've watched you a',
I've been at every beck and ca',
I've wakened ye at mornin' licht,
I've happed ye up in bed at nicht.

"I've shaved ye a' afore ye rose,
Supplied the cloots tae blaw yer nose,
(And may I add in this same verse)
The paper tae, tae dicht yer erse,
But carry on, I'm haunin' ower,
Divide the flamin' thing by fower!"

Sae we got hame, a' freens, och aye!
Eccles and Marr and Young and I.

On winter nichts I whiles luk back,
Far seeing, o'er the distant track,
And dream o' friends I reckon great,
As on through life we watch and wait,
For friendship true is my delight,
And friendship brought us here tonight!

Willie Sharp's New Car

I had a little car for sale,
Which leads me on to tell a tale,
Frien' Willie Sharp frae Minishant,
Decides, "Here's just the car I want."

Now Fraser's garage you'll agree,
Wi' their initials, A & D,
Are members of the Westfield group,
But Willie landed in the soup.

The car delivered then and there,
Was cleaned and polished fair and square,
Hence Mrs Sharp says "Listen son,
We'll make communion oor first run."

Now Willie wi' his troosers pressed,
And Mrs Sharp in Sunday best,
Into this Morris car proceed,
To drink the wine and break the breid.

Though tyres were a' in richt guid fettle,
Perchance ane strikes a sherp bit metal,
Or, while Wull's fit was on the throttle,
He maybe clouts an aul' beer bottle.

Doon went the tyre,
A richt blaw oot.
Says Willie's wife,
"We're up the shoot."

Wullie says, "Aye, we're in a guddle,
For every nit's as ticht's a fiddle,"
And though wi' grunts he puffed and blew,
No' ae damnt nit could he unscrew.

The wife! A fairly stout bit stuff,
Cam' oot the motor in the huff,
Stood on the key to move the nit,
But Hell scud tae the shift would it.

Nae kirk they saw nor heard the bell,
They just had a crack atween theirsel',
I'm sorry folks tae write this line,
Because that caur he bocht was mine!

A Comprehensive Thanks

This social night in freendship's name,
Has shown the star o' Rabbie's fame,
Has made us truly glad we came,
        Tae Castlehill,
Wi' singing hearts we'll toddle hame,
        In richt guidwill.

But ere I bid ye a' adieu,
Some gratitude is justly due,
May I express my thanks to you,
        All joined in one,
Each played their part sincere and true,
        I say, "Well done."

No further praise need I express,
No special names, in singleness,
Each artiste, you must all confess,
        Did quite excel,
Friends, raise the rafters, nothing less,
        Come, - ring the bell.

Advice to Sally

Sometimes, when things get frail and worn,
Your duds get tattered scutched and torn,
You have tae buy new underclaes,
Replacin' togs o' former days.
Noo camisoles are gane lang syne,
And bloomers, that I used tae min',
Some bras you'll ha'e are frayed tae bits,
Get these renewed, for roon your tits,
A tupperware yin, - warm's a pie,
But "Cross my Heart's" a better buy.
Noo Sally, this is my advice,
Silk knickers are a low sale price,
Think a' this oot, my dear freen' Sal,
Signed, - frae an extra special pal.

To Margaret and Davie Raeside

Flitting from West Mainshill to Kirkmichael, 26th October 1995.

You'll ha'e heard o' folks whiles movin',
Frae aroon' the countryside,
You'll ha'e heard o' ithers flittin',
Through the change o' time and tide.
The latest was a flittin',
Just a week or twa since syne,
That day was bleak and poorin',
These are special freens o' mine.

The twenty-sixth October date,
In nineteen ninety-five,
And extra special flittin',
Doon frae West Mainshill did drive,
Ower tae Kirkmichael it did pass,
Tae a braw hoose on the brae,
Baith tired and weary that same nicht,
After a hectic day.

Davie and Margaret, - all the best,
I truly wish for you,
May you baith enjoy retirement,
And health tae see things through.
I pray for sweet contentment,
For the time that's yet to be,
God bless you Dave and Margaret,
With fondest love, frae me.

The Mallard Drake

I am fond of Mother Nature, and of life both wild and tame,
I am happy by the hillside or the glen,
I am fond of winding rivers, and of silent lochs the same,
And I'm very fond of all my fellow-men.

I've a special friend, with nature much alike, his name is Bill,
And he loves all living creatures, great and small,
And, to hurt by word or action, must be sore against his will,
For I truly know, he dearly loves them all.

Then his job, he always tackles in a manner fair and square,
He's the joiner at the mine, - there's lots to do,
You can take it when completed, that a willing hand was there,
And you always may depend, he'll see it through.

Well, it happened in the WInter, there was just a trace of snow,
At this country mine (where lads must earn the pay),
There's a little stream meanders through the hollow down below,
And the water's kind o' slimy I may say.

Now my friend was busy striding to the little powder shed,
(Where the powder's kept, well under lock and key),
When his eye should chance to wander to the streamlet's frozen bed,
Where coot, and water hen, may shelter free.

Now he spotted in an instant, by a little marshy bay,
Where the bank is overhanging by the side,
A Mallard Drake there lurking, with a plumage green and grey,
And beneath a clump of rushes he did glide.

He was forced by bitter Winter to come near the haunts of men,
And to seek some grain of feeding for his wame,
Like the deer that roam the mountains, in the evening seek the glen,
And I reckon, to disturb them, is a shame.

Now this fellow I have mentioned, though a lover of the wild,
Studied drake, so near at hand, he saw the tail,
And I fear his thoughts were ugly, like a cruel hearted child,
Thus, he struck a plan, the way he'd strike a nail.

He decided, with a weapon in his mighty wielding hand,
He could walk the bank, and smartly strike the place,
And the devil showed him plainly, just the stick to do it grand,
And he sallied forth, with murder in his face.

He had marked the spot precisely, where he saw the mallard go,
And he raised the weapon o'er his head on high,
With a most tremendous clatter, he then let him have a blow,
And nothing from the rushes forth did fly.

Then he turned aside the cover, and the drake was lying still,
He was absolutely murdered where he sat,
For his very neck was broken, and you could not see his bill,
Then he lifted him, to see if he was fat.

Then the pang of Conscience struck him, and he felt a stinging pain,
And he wished to God he hadn't done the deed,
And he said he'd give a dollar just to see the bird again,
In the streamlet, where he meant to have a feed.

For in fancy now he saw him, as he paddled to and fro,
And again he saw him clearly in his flight,
And although he took his body to be cooked, I truly know,
That he saw him in his dreams that very night.

And they tell me on the morrow, that he made a plumage neat,
Which he placed upon his darling's Sunday hat,
And the soup was just delicious, and the flesh a perfect treat,
And the bones - they fed the little dog and cat.

Now if you should see a duckling, in the water where you stay,
Or perhaps a little drake go floating by,
Would you like to eat the body, and to throw the bones away,
Well the problem is to kill them - have a try!

Alex. T. Andrew's Testimonial

This nicht in happy freendship met,
This special nicht aside we set,
A presentation to a man,
Held in respect throughoot the lan',
The target made, the honour won,
In unison, we say, "Well done".

The auction mart, doonby in Ayr,
Nae doot, we ken will miss ye sair,
When lamb sales start in fullest swing,
We'll miss ye, in the store sale ring,
Look back with pride these bygone days,
Here's to the future's happy days.

And now I'll look around this crew,
And introduce each man to you.

Willie Parker, quite a star,
Better known aroon Stranraer,
Quite a character as well,
Maybe something like mysel'!

Mr Murdoch, let me say,
Known by letters J and K,
If you haven't met, it's clear,
You're a total stranger here.

One you all must know for sure,
Gavin Hendrie o' the Toor,
Sells great bullocks, big and square,
Often taps the sales in Ayr.

Jimmy Logan, I don't mean,
Yon yin on the tele' screen,
No' the bloke I mean, ava,
Bocht the stuff at Lauder Ha',
Different built I ocht to say,
Mair like Ali - Cassius Clay,
Maxwellton, but no' the braes,
Whaur Annie Laurie spent her days.

Then John Smith weil kent forby,
Lifts yer pair auld deein' kye,
Gies ye five poun' if their guid,
Whiles of coorse just haulf a quid.

Bunty - famous curling guy,
Likes a deal in sheep forby,
Likes tae fish in pool or puddle,
And at time prefers tae guddle.

Willie Murdoch, near at haun',
You can drink as long's your can,
If you canna drive the caur,
You can crawl, it's no' that faur.

John Young bides aboot Kilwinning,
Mony yarns I've heard him spinning,
In the show ring, does the trick,
'Cos they're frichted for his stick.

Hence my freens, it's plain tae see,
There's some heroes at this spree,
Just mysel' - as quate's a moose,
I now hereby introduce,
Though I may be sma' I sweer,
Into wee book gangs guid gear,
May the rafters ring wi' cheer,
That's my wish - true and sincere.

Stair Exhibition

May 1963

The winter, it was long and dour,
And folks were gettin' thrawn and soor,
The spring, nae doot, we a' did ettle,
Wad pit us intae better fettle.
But sad I am tae tell ye a',
The spring was nocht but sleet and snaw,
It was a man, and no' a wuman,
That said the summer wad be comin',
Like weans when promised double ration,
Sae we were gulled wi' expectation,
He said in sunshine we'd be cookin',
When every day we got a drookin'.
Hooever, Stair folk seemed tae rally,
And this man's tale did fairly swally,
They said in Mey, no' ony later,
We'll stagger every normal cratur,
We'll fix a week and stage a show,
And bring the folk baith high and low,
We'll bring them here, baith great and sma',
Frae a' the airts the win' can blaw,
And so it was, on duty bent,
We organised a government,
The party then took up the whip,
And everybody let it rip,
There politics were a' wan then,
For they were "Liberal", this I ken,
We got the tables then and there,
Frae guid kind freens I ken in Ayr.
The shelving, too, we got for - PLEASE -
Frae lads that work wi' honey bees.
We needed cases made o' glass,
So that the folks could freely pass,
And view inside and stand and stare,
At all the beauty lying there,
So that these things they couldna mooch,
Or snaffle in their trooser pooch!
Some boys were bundled off en route,
For Killie's auld Dick Institute,
They brocht back things I'm perfect shair,
Could held a full-grown polar bear.
Says I tae them, "Oh sufferin' jing,
These are for eagles on the wing,

And ere ye start I'll tell ye more,
They'll never keek inside the door,
Turn about lads, and do it quick,
Return these crates to Dirty Dick."
Hooever, we got suited free,
Doon at Carnegie Libraree,
To square the job we lastly made,
And extra special barricade.
The wood for this, you may depend,
Was gifted by a special friend.
Again we landed very lucky,
The roads and pads ootside were mucky,
Our good friend Dormiston for days,
Wi' men and tractors cairted blaze,
They raked the high bits clear o' grevel,
And filled the holes and made them level,
They made a perfect job through-oot,
And gaed it's face a lift nae doot.
Ae morning o' the stinkin' weather,
Wi' boys I'd like a wee bit blether,
Says I, "If you've a load tae spare,
Bung it doon in the field, richt there."
They baith, at aince, said, "In the fiel'!
John Lockhart's certain shair tae squeal."
Says I, "For caurs it's mair invitin',
It's meant tae keep their wheels frae skytin'."
When Willie Thomson, he got crackin',
The papers gave him every backin',
They put in yarns tae fairly suit,
But Willie kens his way aboot,
Wi' lasses, he's a winnin' wey,
He got in screeds and didna pey,
And then the signposts, a' gaen free,
Were fixed up by the R.A.C.,
In case, dear freens, ye werena there,
This "do" was in the manse hall, Stair,
The stuff we had you've no conception,
We had a wonderful collection,
We had a' kin's o' lovely dolls,
Some beauties tae o' Paisley shawls,
We had some bonny cheeny hens,
Auld fashioned dishes, odds an' en's,
A cheeny cock that couldna craw,
An auld clock ca'd a Wag-at-Wa',
Some Christenin' robes for weans langsyne,
And silver, that did fairly shine,

Embroidery din on cloots and towels,
And near a dizen toddy bowls.
For Rabbie Burns we had tae ha'e,
A special corner on display,
A braw wee horse wi' harness on,
A girdle used tae bake the scone,
A pictur' o' an auld time buggy,
And doon below a wooden luggy,
We'd Goering's cap, forby his dagger,
A copper measure used for lager,
Wide at the base, and upward tapers,
Handy for haudin' car'mel papers!
An auld bed warmer wi' a shaft,
Tae me it seems the folk were daft,
Imagine sleepin' soun' wi' yon,
What do you say, Miss Davidson?
Doon in the Kirk where music played,
Were manuscripts and books arrayed,
Communion cups, Communion spoon,
And relics o' dear Jimmy Broon,
A wee, wee bible there on view,
Wi' testaments baith auld and new,
The big ha' bible side by side,
O' auld Scots hames their foremost pride,
And there unscrewed and all fixed up,
A Scottish Covenanter's cup,
Take time and ponder here my son,
On how your heritage was won,
And as you leave the auld kirk door,
Look Heavenward, and wonder more.
Well, all things fixed in grand position,
We opened our great exhibition.
The ladies in the manse got crackin',
And helpers, they were never lackin'.
Miss Wyllie at the door sat doon,
And nabbed aff each yin hauf-a-croon,
There's no' ae person grudged the price,
Because, I tell you, it was nice,
In fact some telt us then and there,
We could hae chairged a tanner mair,
We fed aboot a thoosan' faces,
Frae haunts nearhan' and distant places,
Wi' nice cakestauns and fancy dishes,
We fed them, no' wi' loaves and fishes,
But tattie scones and crumpets neat,
And cakes and buns and biscuits sweet,

And cups o' tea tae wash it doon,
Was that no' chape for hauf-a-croon?
The caurs began tae trickle in,
At twa on Monday efternin,
And so it is they come and go,
To visit this unusual show,
Altho' the caul' win' and the rain,
Wad still hae chilled ye tae the bane,
Wi' wellingtons and macs, we knew,
We'd no' be stuck tae see it through,
We tried tae dae oor best as weel,
To keep the motors oot the fiel'.
Each neuk and corner had a use,
We kept them birlin' roon' the hoose,
Ae day a caur came up the road,
Fu' tae the bung, a tidy load,
The driver was a female sweet,
And stoot, especially roon' the seat!
Says I, "Good afternoon, my dear,
Just put your Austin richt in here."
She placed it perfect to the peg,
As neat, I'd say, as Katie's leg,
Her door just opened half ajar,
'Twas up against another car,
Her heid and shooders managed oot,
But ither bits were faur too stoot,
Says I to her, "Noo dinna worry,
There's nane o' us in ony hurry.
I'll move the culprit ower a bit,
And you'll get oot as sweet's a nit."
Her thanks were so profuse tae me,
I very nearly peyed her tea!
And mony another laugh and joke,
We had among oor ain dear folk,
Although the weather ne'er got kind,
We jogged along and did not mind.
The minister each nicht did snore,
Within this wonder treasure store,
While Mrs Pringle in the manse,
Was merely in a kin' o' trance,
Dreamin' o' burglars in the hut,
Sleepin' wi' only wan e'e shut.
But in the en' when a' was by,
We heaved, nae doot, a heavy sigh,
But gey weel pleased tae feel the stress,
Was crowned indeed wi' huge success.

Far more than cash we gained through this,
In friendship's everlasting bliss.
Each kindness played a living part,
And tuned the pure strings of the heart,
All singing like the birds in May,
We played the game, we won the day.
And love and joy, beyond compare,
Were planted like the flowers, at Stair.

The Lawn Mower

Here Bobby Shearlaw fills the bill,
Aboot lawn mowers at Longhill,
Noo Una Arnott lives richt here,
Takes oot her tools and other gear,
To cut her grass, and tidy through,
And make things look as good as new,
This motor mower would not start,
So she decides with it to part,
She further states (fed up), "I'll chuck it,"
And dump it straight way in the bucket.
A freen, Nairn Brown, a decent chap,
Says, "Una, it is bloody scrap."
Two handy fellows worked wi' Broon,
Nabbed mower, ere the cairt cam' roon.
A lucky prize, they sorted it,
It cut the grass as sweet's a nit,
Cut various lawns, they looked that guid,
Yin says, "It's worth a hunner quid."
'Twas Una's loss - a perfect sin,
For Broon had telt her it was din!

To Mr & Mrs A Reid

On their Ruby Wedding, November 1977.

My dear, and much respected friends,
Life's highway aye has mony bends,
Fair Margaret here, kens that braw weil,
And sae does Andy, dacent chiel,
Aboot the "Bank", and ower the braes,
I've kent them weil fu' mony days,
Up whaur Dalmellington keeks oot,
They pledged their troth, withoot a doot,
That's forty years gane by sin' syne,
Ae week ago, - they'll baith hae min',
When five and twenty years had fled,
They held, richt here, in this homestead,
A silver waddin', yes, richt here,
A nicht o' happy joy and cheer,
My wife and I, and ithers too,
A' met in Nineteen Sixty Two,
I met freen' Andy 'mong the coos,
He luks their mooths, - their tits he pu's,
Each Tuesday, he's the man tae get,
It saves you sen'in' for the vet.
On Thursdays tae, the stores gang roon,
He's dottin' a' the numbers doon,
"I've six wee bullocks, Andy son,
I think I'll sell them one by one."
"If you had yin tae sell - dear me,
You'd hauf the bloody thing," says he.
I smile, and take it, hence that means,
We're still the very best o' freens.
Anither fifteen years is through,
And here, we're at anither DO,
Some faces noo we dinna see,
That were weil kent at that last spree.
We've shed for some a silent tear,
Big chinges, freens, in fifteen year.
Yet life moves on frae day to day,
Some, like masel', are gie and grey.
Well Margaret lass, and Andy, freen',
I hope you're spared tae see the scene,
Perhaps in this self same hotel,
I'll come again and wish ye well,
And through the next ten years I'll sing,
Till Golden Wedding Bells shall ring.

B.M.C. Burns Supper

The British Motor Corporation,
Have formed a club of reputation,
A Driver's Club, throughout the nation,
        To do good turns,
This nicht, met in commemoration,
        O' Rabbie Burns.

Since we are brithers great or small,
Within this famous Bakers Hall,
The Lasses Toast, this is my call,
        Worthwhile indeed,
I'll liken lasses, young and aul',
        Tae scones and breid.

The loaf that's stale, and never reeks,
That's hard, that's lay aboot for weeks,
Is like a dame wi' long thick breeks,
        Low doon her thigh,
Where as the loaf the driver seeks,
        Is warm as pie.

The swells that rin aboot the street,
Wi' silken panties roon their seat,
These are the yins that can't be beat,
        Dae you agree?
And winkle pickers on their feet,
        You're tellin' me.

Oh some are dark and some are fair,
And some hae curlers in their hair,
And some wi' scent pollute the air,
        As sure as fate,
And some, although they're no' a' there,
        Still want a date.

You've got tae watch their passin' fancies,
They gie sic shy like, tender glances,
They'll lure ye intae slow gaun dances,
        And rope ye in,
They've got tae mak' sic bold advances,
        Their rent's ahin.

Tak' Christine, though she was rale cute,
They've shut her in, I raither doot,
They've squared her tail, she's up the shoot,
        She lies on boards,
Insteed o' on some peer, frae oot
        The Hoose o' Lords.

But ither lasses they unfold,
A hert that's never ever cold,
A love that's true, to have and hold,
        If you'll but share,
They're truly worth their weight in gold,
        And even mair.

Faur be it lads for me tae boast,
Withoot the lasses, we'd be lost,
Especially, roon this Ayrshire coast,
        Weil bred and braw,
Staun up then lads, and drink this toast,
        God bless them a'.

To 'Tot'

on her Eightieth Birthday, 6th December 1979.

It is wi' pride and joy nae doot,
To you this nicht we all salute,
A birthday party, great and good,
We celebrate at Meiklewood.
'Tis eighty years I ocht tae say,
Since you, dear lass, saw licht o' day,
Weil can I min' when we were weans,
Park o' Barneigh and Monkwood Mains,
Weil can I min', and this is true,
The nichts I've even slept wi' you,
I min' The Park a' ins and oots,
Doon in the pond I guddled troots,
And then at Monkwood Mains, in turn,
I girned them often in the burn,
I min' ye as a bonnie bride,
Later at Mains ye cam tae bide,
I min' the flittin', by and by,
Wi' horse and lorry through Dalry.
These are the days this nicht we min',
The happy days o' auld lang syne,
An eightieth birthday, this is why,
We're lookin' back on days gane by,
But forward we maun cast an e'e,
And reckon wi' the yet to be.
May health and joy, from heaven sent,
Be yours, dear Tot, and sweet content,
These wishes, heartfelt and sincere,
Are penned, with love for you, my dear.

If only we...

If only we, on each new day,
When getting out of bed could say:
"What is there now that I might do,
As this old world I ramble through,
To make things better where I can,
For someone, just a fellow man?"

If only we would smile and say,
Good morning, though the sky be grey,
Take up the pen, a letter send,
To one, a long-forgotten friend,
Or by some sick bed sit and read,
Of kindness, keep on sowing seed.

If it were done without delay,
How rich a dividend 'twould pay,
In happiness for one and all,
Whether in cottage or in hall,
All this and more, you're sure to find,
If only you'd make up your mind.

Love

Love girds the distant foreign sphere,
And spans the world around,
Love lends an ever listening ear,
To every tuneful sound,
And how the heart bounds light with glee,
For friends both tried and true,
Though parted by the angry sea,
I'll aye remember you.

Letter to Messrs D.W. Shaw & Company

Solicitors, 24 Sandgate Ayr. This reply was sent following a letter from the solicitors demanding the fee of £5.00 for castrating a bull sold by Allan to James Marr, Cruachan, Minishant. Allan, however, knew that the "bull" was in fact a bullock, castrated twice!

Dear Sirs, I write with haste to say,
I had your note of yesterday,
I answer letters by return,
Unless, of course, the ones I burn.
In this sad case it would appear,
Your client thought he bought a steer,
Discounting every market rule,
This steer turns out to be a bull,
This truly criminal contravention,
Was perpetrated with intention,
A downright trick, and quite uncanny,
This rogue would do his bloomin' granny.
Thus states your client in distress,
And dancin' like a bear, I guess.
Well, well, I'm not perturbed, indeed,
At times like this I keep the heid,
If Mr Marr, or me, or you,
Had got what this poor beast came through,
We would be truly in distress,
And simply useless, more or less,
Write him and tell him right away,
That I cannot see my way to pay,
And also tell him he's a fool,
To think a harmless steer's a bull!
To this five quid I mean to stick,
Sincerely yours, "Dunkitterick".